THE CRESTLINE SERIES

Donald F. Wood

MBI Publishing Company

Dedication
To Art Wallace, Dean, College of Business,
San Francisco State University from 1993–1998

First published in 1998 by MBI Publishing Company, 729 Prospect Avenue, PO Box 1, Osceola, WI 54020-0001 USA

© Donald F. Wood, 1998

MBI Publishing Company books are also available at discounts in bulk quantity for industrial or sales-promotional use. For details write to Special Sales Manager at Motorbooks International Wholesalers & Distributors, 729 Prospect Avenue, Osceola, WI 54020-0001 USA.

Library of Congress Cataloging-in-Publication Data
Wood, Donald F.
    American buses/Donald F. Wood.
        p. cm.—(Crestline series)
    Includes index.
    ISBN 0-7603-0432-7 (pbk.:alk. paper)
    1. Buses—United States—History. I. Title. II. Series.
TL232.W66   1998
629.222'33'0973—dc21   98-34962

On the front cover: For over 80 years, Greyhound has been America's pre-eminent intercity bus company. This beautifully restored mid-1950s GMC-built Greyhound coach is a rolling reminder of Greyhound's glory days when the company and its affiliates operated over 5,000 vehicles. *David Gooley*

On the back cover: A collection of three wonderful buses, from the top. An early 1920s White that was used by the Hollywood Golf and Country Club in Florida. *Florida Photographic Archives, Strozier Library, Florida State University* A 1964 Ford with a Superior school bus body. *Superior Coach Division, Sheller Globe Corporation* An articulated, early 1990s North American Bus Industries bus used by theMiami-Dade Transit Agency. *Bobbie C. Crichton*

Edited by Anne T. McKenna

Designed by Todd Sauers

Printed in the United States of America

CONTENTS

ACKNOWLEDGMENTS

A number of individuals assisted, and I thank them for their help and hold them blameless for our mistakes. They include: Kenneth E. Anderson, Star Trax Celebrity Coach; Tim Anderson, MICO, Inc.; Kathy T. Armstrong, Blue Bird Corporation; Robert A. Burrowes; Elisabeth Chrétien, Prevost Car Inc.; C. J. Collins, Cable Car Classics; Bobbie C. Crichton, Miami-Dade Transit; Patrice Gauvin, Nova Bus Corporation; Susan L. Gerlach, Transpec Worldwide; Rich Himes, North American Bus Industries; Sue Hodge, Tri-Met; Lora Kjensrud, World Trans, Inc.; Jennifer Kuschmider, Kent State University; Ben Leonard, Phoenix Public Transit Department; Frank Lichtanski, Monterey-Salinas Transit; Joseph W. McBride, Kansas City (Missouri) Aviation Department; John H. McKane, The Pacific Bus Museum; Wally Mellor; associated students at University of California at Davis; Sandra Metellus, Port Authority of New York & New Jersey; Kathy Miller, Carpenter Industries; Rich Nelson, San Francisco State University; David Norton; Ernesto Olivarez, San Francisco State University; Lou Parsons, Orion Bus Industries; Ethel L. Pattison, Los Angeles Department of Airports; Larry Plachno, National Bus Trader, Inc.; Michael Rea, West County Transportation Agency; Bob Redden; Mary R. Schmidt, Broward County Mass Transit Division; Nancy Sites, Baltimore/Washington International Airport; Cheryl D. Soon, Honolulu Department of Transportation Services; Steve Tarter, Greater Peoria Mass Transit District; Mary Tradii, Denver Regional Transportation District; Jules Tygiel, San Francisco State University; Athena Valis, MCI; Christoph von der Osten, Setra; Phyllis Vanistendal, Philadelphia International Airport; and Bill West.

I thank all the sources of photographs who, we hope, are accurately covered in the credit lines. Some limited help was found on the World Wide Web, but given the transitory nature of many references there, they will not be directly cited. Some of the useful subject titles referenced there were: "Bus Drivers and School Bus Drivers," "Buses and Air Quality," "Buses of Yesteryear," "Chattanooga's Electric Bus Initiative: story ideas," "Elvis Presley's Tour Bus," "Frank W. Cyr, 'Father of the Yellow School Bus,'" "History of Mass Transit in Williamsport," "Motor Bus Society," "Motorcoach Industry Fact Sheet," "Neoplan City Buses," "Remembering Life on the Tortoise," "The Montgomery Bus Boycott: 1956," "The story about the Martha White Bus," "Traveling by Tortoise," and "Welcome to Bus Depot on the Net's Buses in Northern America." Another useful source of information, not itemized in the bibliography, was literature from chassis and bus body builders, some dating as early as the 1920s.

Several persons generously support a fund at San Francisco State University that assists old truck research. I acknowledge some of the donors: Stuart B. Abraham, Edward C. Couderc of Sausalito Moving & Storage, Gene Bills, Gilbert Hall, David Kiely, ROADSHOW, Gene Olson, Oshkosh Truck Foundation, Art Van Aken, Charlie Wacker, Bill West, and Fred Woods. Several chapters of the American Truck Historical Society have also provided financial support to the program at San Francisco State University. The chapters include: Central Coast of California, Hiawathaland, Inland Empire, Mason-Dixon, Metro Jersey, Minnesota Metro, Music City, Northeast Ohio, Shenandoah Valley, and Southern Michigan.

Donald F. Wood
San Francisco State University

INTRODUCTION

When researching buses, several differences in terminology will arise. No single definition encompasses all that a bus is thought to be. The term "bus" is probably derived from "omnibus," which comes from the Latin word "omnis," meaning every or all. Early in this century it was often spelled "buss." Many federal government publications define a bus as a motor vehicle designed to carry 10 or more passengers. The common usage of the word has come to mean a large motor-driven passenger vehicle operating usually in accordance to a schedule along a fixed route.

Buses have had a huge impact on the "comings and goings" of America. From transporting people in cities to and from their jobs every morning, to getting children to school each day, buses have provided an efficient and economical method of transportation. And for those wishing to see the vast beauty of America, buses have provided the opportunity at a reasonable cost.

Besides city dwellers, small-town America is especially dependent on buses. Sometimes the bus is the only option for transportation, since the airlines and Amtrak tend to serve mainly metropolitan areas. In these many thousands of communities, people without access to automobiles must rely on buses for connections to the outside world.

In addition to providing transportation across America, buses have also served another purpose—a communication link between many parts of the country. In small-town America, the bus station was also the newsstand, since newspapers and magazines were delivered by bus. If you wanted to know the latest headline news, the bus station was the place to be.

Although there are numerous types of buses, the most common are those in regular passenger-carrying service. These buses differ according to the type of market they service. Local transit buses make many stops and starts and during peak hours have many standees. Suburban bus systems have more spacious and comfortable seating and no or few standees. Intercity buses carry passengers long distances and attempt to compete with passenger trains and airlines in terms of space and passenger comfort. Intercity buses are sometimes referred to as coaches. In the industry, the word "coach" is used to upgrade the image of a bus. Travel brochures commonly say that passengers will be carried by motor coach, rather than bus. At one time the word "stage" was used for intercity or rural operations.

Intercity buses often also carry freight, in addition to passengers. Some intercity bus vehicles were built with bulkheads on the main floor, with the area in front devoted to passengers and the area in back to freight. Literature from the S. S. Albright Company in Sacramento in 1930 pictured a White chassis with the caption reading: "combination passenger and freight van—this bus has room for eight passengers in front and room

An early 1920s White used in Tampa. Florida Photographic Archives

The familiar school bus, a 1938 Ford with a Gillig school bus body. Gillig Corp.

in rear for about 1 1/2 tons of freight." Some archival photos show truck bodies with what appear to be removable seats. It's believed that those were used by firms as temporary buses for their own workers as well as for carrying products at other times. European bus builders in the 1930s sometimes built two interchangeable bodies for a single truck chassis, one for carrying freight, the other for carrying passengers. They did this because of very high per-vehicle taxes.

School buses are immediately recognizable by their yellow-orange color. However, if you take a closer look, you'll notice that not all school buses look the same. There are a variety of chassis and body arrangements. Traditionally, truck chassis were used with a bus body mounted behind the engine and cowl. However, some buses place the driver and controls at the very front, where visibility is better. Today, some school buses are smaller and have lifts so that they can transport disabled children. This book devotes a considerable amount of space to school buses because of their historic significance. In the first half of the century, buses aided in rural school consolidation, which led to the decline of many tiny settlements in rural America. Since the late 1950s, school buses have been used in many cities to promote racial integration in schools. The term "busing" was used to describe this urban process. School

buses are by far the largest group of buses in terms of number of vehicles.

Another type of bus is the jitney. This is a vehicle that is a cross somewhere between a bus and a taxicab. Peter Pan Bus Lines of Massachusetts started business in 1933, using three drivers who made two round trips a day from Springfield to Boston. At that time, the conventional Buick sedans they used were referred to as jitneys. On San Francisco's busy Mission Street, jitneys are vans that are privately owned, which pick up and discharge passengers. They charge fares and compete with both conventional transit buses and the Bay Area Rail Transit (BART), the area's heavy rail transit system. According to an article in the July 28, 1997, issue of the *San Francisco Chronicle*, there is only one jitney left in the city, a faded 25-seat 1978 GMC bus.

The hotel bus had its origin in horse-drawn rigs, used to carry hotel patrons between rail stations and the hotel's lobby. Hotels in cities, small towns, and resort areas competed among themselves. As motorized vehicles became available, hotels began providing bus service from the rail station to their lobby, similar to today's "courtesy vans" provided by airport motels. One can accurately assume that some bus operators solicited passengers stepping off trains to patronize their hotel. Often the hotel buses would back up to the rail station platform and load from the rear. Seating was longitudinal, along the buses' sides. A baggage rack was available, although sometimes the travelers' trunks would be carried in a separate wagon or truck. A second use for hotel buses was to carry hotel guests from one site to another on the hotel grounds. Some early hotel buses were referred to as a "Tally Ho"—a name once used for horse-drawn pleasure coaches.

Tour buses carry passengers to see various sites and tourist attractions in a city, or across the country. Almost every city has anywhere from 2 to 20 different half- or full-day tour bus excursions available. There are also bus tours that last several days, with overnight lodging in hotels. In gambling states, casinos often subsidize tour bus operations that deliver customers to their doors on an excursion.

One very useful type of bus is as a work crew bus. For as long as there have been workers to move from job site to job site, there have been work crew buses to do the job. One principle of transportation is to consolidate in order to conserve resources. It was cheaper to send a larger number of workers in a single vehicle. Some work crew buses carried workers between their dwellings and a single job site; others carried workers between job sites. Prior to World War II, an employer could not assume that all of his workers had their own automobiles. However, after the war, as automobile ownership became more widespread, it was less essential for the

Designer Alexis de Sakhnoffsky was retained by White in the mid-1930s to develop streamlined bodies for White trucks. This is his concept, drawn in 1936 for a "dream coach of 1950." National Automotive History Collection, Detroit Public Library

employer to provide transportation for workers. Yet issues of work force control and liability for employees traveling in their own vehicles still made it advisable to use buses in some situations.

Work buses took many forms. There were stretched autos, vans, modified truck bodies, or conventional city or over-the-road buses. For many years, the Detroit Fire Department ran "flying squads" of firemen who would be rushed in buses to the scene of large fires to reinforce the firemen already at the blaze. Utility companies have maintenance workers traveling from site to site using trucks equipped with "crew cabs," similar to four-door sedans, to carry larger groups of workers. Some of the larger police departments use buses to carry policemen to sites where extra reinforcement is needed. Security services may use buses to spot guards at night and to pick them up in the morning. Stevedore companies use buses to carry workers from hiring halls to shipside. Sports teams often have their own buses for carrying the players. In a few instances, the work bus is a form of an employee benefit. Workers who must work at night may be promised bus delivery to and from their home, or parked auto. Some shopping centers and airports that are short of parking space do not allow employees to park in their main lots, but rather at a more distant lot, and then be carried back and forth by bus.

Besides an actual bus, there are many vehicles with various names, which perform the traditional duties of a bus—transporting people. One such example is a van. Vans can be either a goods-carrying truck or a squarish passenger-carrying body on a light truck chassis. Currently, passenger vans are available with a capacity of up to 15 passengers. "Hack" is a term that usually refers to taxicabs. Yet some Navistar photographs from 1920 show a fleet of International school buses with hinged signs on the side saying: "School Hack." A tram is a small cart, usually one of a series, pulled by a tractor. Trams are commonly used at amusement parks or on plant tours. Usually, trams are not intended for opera-

tion on public roads and highways. Station wagons are vehicles with an automobile or light truck chassis. When passenger loads are very light, sometimes a bus operator might use a station wagon instead to transport passengers. Taxicabs generally have passenger car bodies, and they represent the smallest vehicles used as "for-hire" passenger service.

Stretched autos or stretched limousines are auto bodies on chassis that have been strengthened and lengthened to carry one or more additional seats. They look like a conventional sedan except that they are longer and have additional bench seats and side doors.

A Doodlebug is a bus that is outfitted with railroad wheels and runs on railroad tracks. Most carried passengers, but photographs can be found of some carrying passengers in an auto body at the front and pulling a freight car behind.

When taking a look at buses, the concept of ownership arises. The vast majority today are in public ownership, either municipal transit agencies or school districts, although some school districts contract with private firms to provide the service. The term "property" refers to the bus (or rail) operating agency. A charter bus is one that is loaned by its owner to another party, although often the owner supplies the driver and fuel.

Besides providing transportation, buses have various uses due to their spacious bodies. The most common examples are traveling stores and classrooms. Bend, Oregon, used a 1954 Flxible bus chassis and body to carry ladders. It had been built using racks and ladders from a retired city service truck. The bus body was used to keep the ladders dry. This bus stayed in service until 1980. The Thomas bus building company, located in High Point, North Carolina, builts "poultry buses," used to carry caged poultry, taking advantage of the bus body's spacious interior dimensions. Retired buses sometimes continue to lead active lives by being outfitted with living accommodations and converted into a traveling home. These are often called private coaches. New buses are also used for private coaches. The bus builder supplies the chassis and "shell" to the outfitter.

Bus development can be traced over time, as is done in this book, on a decade-by-decade basis. This approach yields "thick" chapters for those decades when there were many new models offered. James and Genevieve Wren in *Motor Trucks of America* said that in 1924, there were more than 125 different types of buses built by the truck and bus industry. By way of contrast, in the mid-1960s, the number of bus builders shrank to a handful, some of which were building school bus bodies only.

In the book, manufacturers are specified when known. In some cases, truck builders supplied the chassis and bus body builders completed the bus bodies.

A MACK BUS SALESMAN'S DREAM . . .

This 1944 ad was entitled: "A Mack Bus Salesman's Dream." The rig is propelled by rockets. Mack Museum

Some bus manufacturers built the entire vehicle. Bus building methods changed over time. Four books are recommended for readers interested in specific bus manufacturers. The books are: G. N. Georgano, *The Complete Encyclopedia of Commercial Vehicles*; Albert Mroz, *The Illustrated Encyclopedia of American Trucks and Commercial Vehicles*; Larry Plachno, *Modern Intercity Coaches*; and Ed Stauss, *The Bus World Encyclopedia of Buses*. The latter two deal with the period since about 1950.

This book covers the decades of the twentieth century. The topic is very large and this book does not attempt to be encyclopedic. There are cases when a topic will be mentioned in one chapter and not raised again even though it might fit into any one of several decades. During the twentieth century, two factors affected the role of buses. The first is the rise of the automobile, with all its accompanying technology and massive, paved highway system built to serve it. Second is the decline—and near disappearance—of rail passenger transportation including local, interurban, and intercity rail service.

In terms of numbers, the federal government estimates that there were just under 700,000 buses in the United States in 1996. Of these, an estimated 570,000 are school buses, higher than the industry's estimate of 413,000, which apparently covered only buses used for carrying students to and from kindergarten through 12th grade public schools. Local transit agencies operated about 67,000 full-size buses and 28,000 smaller "demand-responsive" buses. The federal government itself operated 5,000 buses. The remaining buses were tour buses and intercity transit buses. (Private/public ownership is hard to determine; some public agencies contract with private firms to provide public service.)

A number of statistics presented throughout the book are not always consistent with one another. Most were taken from contemporary sources. There are several reasons for inconsistencies such as the changing urban boundaries and switches between public and private ownership and control.

In the pages that follow there is no single thread of development. Buses evolved according to the necessity of performing specific tasks. Sometimes there was some overlapping, often there was not.

CHAPTER ONE

1901-1910

The automobile's origins date to the late nineteenth century. At the turn of the century, the automobile was regarded as little more than a curiosity. But by 1910, the automobile was well on its way to becoming a part of mainstream America. However, it's highly unlikely that the same could be said for motorized buses at the time.

Two highlights of this early decade reported by Wren and Wren were the introduction of the first White bus in 1904, and the use of flanged wheels on an automobile that carried passengers for hire on the Sierra Railroad in California.

In 1905, Mack delivered its first gasoline rail motor car to a 3-foot gauge railroad in Colorado. In that same year, the Fifth Avenue Coach Line introduced bus service to New York City.

During this decade, the transportation offerings were many. Passengers living in a city were served by electric streetcars. In major urban

"Observation Automobile" is painted on the side of this circa-1906 electric with elevated seating. The William F. Harrah Automobile Foundation

areas, electric "interurbans" also supplied service to and from suburbs, with more comfortable and more spacious seating, and few stops. Between cities, a massive network of railroads operated many passenger trains, and offered good, frequent service to most areas of the United States. Horse-drawn rigs were used to carry passengers between rail stations and hotels, although just after the turn of the century, electric buses replaced horses in this assignment. Excursion buses were some of the first to be motorized, in part because their routes covered areas less likely to have streetcar service. On the Great Lakes and along the ocean shores, passengers had the option of boat service as well.

Harvey Firestone Jr. in *Man on the Move*, wrote, "By 1909, two automobiles were covering the 100 miles between San Angelo and Big Springs, Texas, daily, carrying United States mail and passengers."

A trade publication published in the 1970s by the National Association of Motor Bus Owners reminisced about the beginning days:

Early bus drivers and passengers often had to be hardy, to say the least. In subzero weather, passengers in primitive vehicles were provided lap robes and even hot bricks. A side result was scorched upholstery. Roads were narrow and more often than not were no more than rough gravel or crushed stone. Speeds thus were slow and rest stops frequent. If a tire went flat, it might be necessary to ride the rim to the next destination. The story is told of one pioneer operator who had a route that at one point frequently developed an impassable mud hole. He solved that by arranging his schedules so that buses from opposite ends of the line met at the mud hole. Passengers and their baggage were then transferred across the hole by a temporary foot bridge, the buses turned around and the trips were completed..

A 1907 Auto-Car electric with a 14-passenger bus body. Auto-Cars were built in Buffalo, New York; this company should not be confused with the firm that built the more well-known Autocar trucks. The entrance was at the rear, and there was a baggage rail on top. Two Westinghouse motors propelled the rig at 15 miles per hour. Free Library of Philadelphia

In 1908, this electric tour bus was used in the nation's capital. It has plush individual seats. Note lattice-type roof to support a tarp. American Automobile Manufacturers Assn.

A circa-1908 Mack sightseeing bus with the steering wheel located on the right side. The tour guide had his own seat in front, facing the passengers. The original white ink caption says "sight-seeing car passing the north entrance to the Iveywood extension." The William F. Harrah Automobile Foundation

Used in Gray's Harbor, Washington, this bus had a door that opened in front. Oregon Historical Society

The words "Knickerbacker Hall Kindergarten" are painted on the side of this 1909 Overland, which has what looks like a dog catcher's body. Shortly after this period, Overland would become associated with Willys. National Automotive History Collection, Detroit Public Library

This 1910 Buick bus was powered by a 22-horsepower engine. Smithsonian Institution

Lauth-Juergens trucks were built in Chicago, then in Fremont, Ohio. This Lauth-Juergens, circa 1910, has an enclosed bus body. Hendrickson Mfg. Co.

This Mack from about 1910 was used as a tour bus. National Automotive History Collection, Detroit Public Library

A circa-1910 Packard with right-hand steering. The sign on top says "Crystal Park." Packard built trucks until 1923. American Automobile Manufacturers Assn.

CHAPTER TWO

1911-1920

Firestone described the origins of two major bus operators in 1912: "a jobless miner named J. T. Hayes bought himself a secondhand Model T Ford and began driving people back and forth between San Diego and El Centro, California. He met his San Diego passengers in front of the Pickwick Theater, so he called his little company "Pickwick Stages."

In 1914, a Hupmobile dealer in Hibbing, Minnesota, who was unable to sell the Hupmobile touring car he had in stock, squeezed some extra seats into it, and began a schedule of trips between Hibbing and a nearby town. This one-time Hupmobile dealer was named Carl Eric Wickham, and he is the acknowledged founder of Greyhound bus lines, the nation's dominant intercity carrier.

This is also the decade when "jitneys" flourished. A 1915 publication of the American Electric Railroad Association, entitled *Cost of Service of the Jitney Bus*, said, "There has been, and still is, no uniformity among the cars engaging in the "jitney" service. They range in size from the ubiquitous Ford, carrying four passengers, through all the larger and heavier makes to especially built double-deck cars carrying upwards of 20 passengers. By far the largest number, however, are Ford touring cars, and following these come second-hand pleasure cars, seating four, five, or six passengers."

Brian Richards, in *The Taxi: Transport for the Future? The Taxi Project: Realistic Solutions for Today*, wrote:

Avery trucks were built in Peoria, Illinois. The passenger body on this 1911 Avery truck had capacity for 17 passengers. During inclement weather, the truck had "curtains." The caption said: "Showing Special Passenger Truck with Curtains enclosing the Sides, Rear and Front." Whether and how willingly passengers traveled inside the enclosed curtains was not specified. The William F. Harrah Automobile Foundation

In 1914 in Los Angeles, along the streetcar routes, driver-owned Ford Model Ts cruised picking up often five or more passengers waiting at the [streetcar] stops. Thus began a shared-taxi operation named "jitney." In some cities, such as Detroit and Bridgeport, jitneys carried as many as half the streetcar passengers at the peak hour, and one journal estimated that by 1915, some 62,000 jitneys were in operation across the country. Seattle, for example, had over 500 jitneys carrying 40,000 passengers a day.

Streetcar operators were alarmed at this loss of business and persuaded state and local governments to pass restrictions of jitneys so severe, that in most markets, jitneys were eliminated by 1920.

However, now the motor bus began making inroads into streetcar traffic. Grover Whalen wrote in 1920 that the streetcars' fixed routes were a cause of congestion, while "In contrast with this rigid, unaccommodating system, the motor bus is a flexible operation. It adjusts itself to traffic, swings around a slower vehicle, is not impeded, does not impede. It speeds up the traffic, rather than hindering it."

The automobile played a huge role in the evolution of the bus. Indeed, the transition from private auto to cab, to jitney, to bus, was merely one of passenger-carrying capacity. Many small bus operations started using

A 1912-13 White used in New Jersey by the New Brunswick Bus Line. Volvo/White

automobiles, and automobiles were often used for routes with small numbers of passengers.

The stretched automobile had origins along three different avenues. First was the so-called commercial chassis. Nearly all automakers offered a commercial chassis, which consisted of an auto chassis with sheet metal as far back as the cowl or including the windshield, front doors, and driver's seat. Vehicles would be purchased this way and then shipped to a body builder, who would complete a limousine body, a truck body, or a bus body, and deliver it to a customer. Auto manufacturers also often marketed lines of light or medium trucks that shared sheet metal in the front with the auto. Sometimes this also involved providing a chassis with a longer wheelbase for truck and bus operations.

Lastly, in the period from about 1915 until 1925, many kits were sold for extending the frames of automobiles, primarily the Ford Model T. There was once a thriving business in kits for converting autos to trucks, with at least a dozen firms offering such kits. The Ford T's kit helped strengthen and lengthen the frame. The rear hubs were fitted with chain-drive sprockets and linked by chain drive to a new, heavier rear axle located farther back than it had been on the automobile. The best-known maker was probably the Smith Form-a-Truck Co. of Chicago.

An alternative to the chain drive was to add a longer driveshaft. The Hudford Company of Philadelphia, which later changed its product name to Truxton, was a major manufacturer of this feature. Truxton ads claimed that their product could make units with up to two tons of capacity, and either 126-inch or 138-inch wheelbases. The buyer also had gear ratio options as he chose the gear axle.

Sales literature from the Motor-Accessory Distributing Co. of Boston, which sold "Longford" auto parts, lists a kit that included:

. . . two extension side frames, two spring leaves, four rear spring clips, one rear axle truss rod, one shaft

extension support, one Longford extension drive shaft set, two running board brackets, one running board brace rod, two standards for side frame truss rods, two side frame truss rods, two brake rod extensions, two side mud pans, two running boards, one tail-light bracket, 15 cotter pins, one rear spring hanger, 35 rivets and 36 bolts.

Still another firm was the Xtend-Ford Company of Philadelphia. Their kits included running board extensions, aprons that fitted above the running board up to the bottom of the body, and rear commercial fenders. The Dearborn Motortruck Company of Chicago built the chain-drive "Dearborn Truck Attachment" for Fords, but their ads show them attached to Cadillac, Maxwell, Buick, Mitchell, Chalmers, Buick, Cole, Hudson, Overland, and Packard automobile chassis. Their ads offered four kits: the $350 kit converted a Ford into a one-ton truck; the $400 kit converted any other make into a one-ton truck; the $450 kit converted a Ford into a two-ton truck; and the $500 kit converted any other car into a two-ton truck. There is not much information about these kits after 1925. Ford began producing a truck chassis, the TT, in 1917. The trucks are discussed because they indicate a response to the demand for lengthening and strengthening the automobile's frame. Individuals building passenger-carrying vehicles would probably be more interested in using extended automobile frames because of the trim and extra comfort features, as well as the likelihood that they could purchase additional seats and doors from the firms who supplied the auto manufacturer. The result was a vehicle that looked like an elongated automobile.

Transportation historians often consider 1916 as the year when U.S. railroads reached their ultimate peak. They would never become any larger. World War I would strain them to the point that a government takeover was necessary. Their decline was to continue for nearly the remainder of the century. What is significant is that as railroad passengers decreased, the railroads did little or nothing to stop it. This left the passenger market wide open for automobiles, airplanes, and of course, buses.

In 1919, Delaware and Wyoming became the last of the then 48 states to authorize public funds to be used for transporting school pupils.

Bus industry developments during the decade reported by Wren and Wren include a rash of transit strikes, which led private automobile owners to become "jitneys," offering rides at five cents each. Trucks were also pressed into jitney service, using wooden soap boxes as seats. In 1918, California began regulating its motor bus industry in terms of rates, safety, and designated market areas, and curbing the use of jitneys.

"Tally-Ho," a term usually associated with hotel buses, is painted on this early Packard. National Automotive History Collection, Detroit Public Library

The American Livery & Stage Co. of Ferndale, California, used this circa-1912 White. It had right-hand steering, a bulb horn, and poles in place for holding a top. The side step was hinged and is shown in folded position. Volvo/White

A White Automobile Co. dealership can be seen in the background behind a 1912 White used in Modena, Utah. The graphics on the glass noted that the company offered both touring cars and trucks. *Volvo/White*

The Hesse Body Company of Kansas City outfitted this circa-1913 Mack with a combination passenger and freight carrying body. Note the words "Bus Line" on side panels of the wagon box. *Hesse Corporation*

The Tacoma Transit Company in Tacoma, Washington, used this 1914 White with a "modern" appearing body. The top windows opened for ventilation. *Volvo/White*

Atterburys were built in Buffalo, New York. This circa-1915 Atterbury has a 20-passenger "tourist" body. *The William F. Harrah Automobile Foundation*

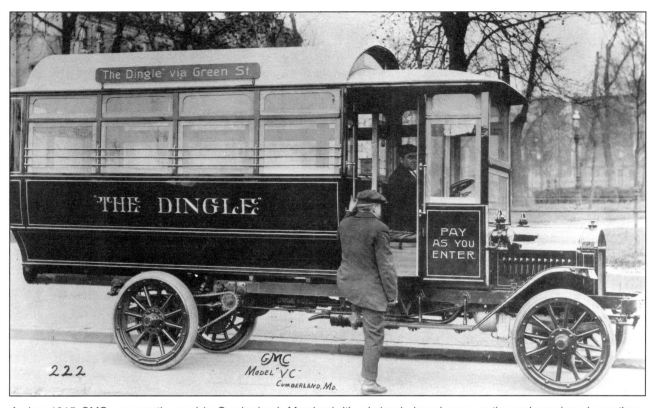

A circa-1915 GMC, apparently used in Cumberland, Maryland. It's obviously brand new, as the undercarriage is spotless. *Kelly-Springfield*

This circa-1915 Service chassis had a 12-passenger bus body. One of the truck's listed features was electric lights. Service trucks were built in Wabash, Indiana. *Wabash County Historical Museum*

San Francisco's Hotel Whitcomb used this 1915 White 12-passenger bus to meet passengers at the rail station or ferry terminal. Note that passengers board from the rear. *Volvo/White*

This pre-World War I White bus had bench seats on each side of the interior. Steering is on the right and the windshield opens for ventilation. *National Tour Association*

A 1916 White with an enclosed door. The snaps along the sill are for holding snap-down side curtains. Note the hinged step by the entrance. *Volvo/White*

An extended frame 1917 Stude-baker, with an enclosed body. The vehicle shown has only one headlight, no doubt a temporary condition. *The William F. Harrah Automobile Foundation*

This bus was used near Canton, Ohio, and has 1917 taxi plates. *The Hoover Co., North Canton, Ohio*

Off to the races at Hialeah are these circa-World War I White buses. *Florida Photographic Archives*

S. S. Albright Co., a Sacramento body builder, constructed this open body with four rows of seats behind the driver on what is probably a Dodge chassis. *California State Library*

The hotel bus body was built by McCabe-Powers, a long-time body builder in St. Louis, who recently went out of business. This is a late 'teens Ford. *McCabe-Powers Body Co.*

Traveling along a rutted rural road is this World War I-vintage International with a Giant school bus body. It has 1919 Iowa license plates. Giant was located in Council Bluffs, Iowa. *Giant Manufacturing Co.*

During a transit strike in New York City just after World War I, trucks were pressed into service to carry people to and from work. This one looks like it's at full capacity. *Manufacturers Hanover Trust Company*

This shows how an open sedan body would be stretched. The darker areas on either end are the original body and doors. The lighter material is wood, and we can see where doors, side panels, and a roof have been added. *New Haven Carriage & Auto Works, Portland, Oregon*

Built on a Ford T chassis, this rig carried passengers and freight on rail tracks between Newport and Waldport, Oregon. *Lincoln County Historical Society, Newport, Oregon*

This wooden school bus body was built by Superior on a 1920 Garford chassis. The bottom halves of door panels have wire mesh inside of glass. Both Garford trucks and Superior bodies were built in Lima, Ohio. *Superior Coach Division, Sheller Globe Corporation*

A circa-1920 GMC operated by a Cleveland moving company. The sides folded down and the rig was also rented out for outings such as "hay rides." The lettering at bottom says "Buss parties," and readers over 80 years old know that "buss" is synonymous with "kiss." *Wm. Fridrich Moving & Storage*

This circa-1922 Locomobile on an extended chassis operated between Portland and Salem, Oregon. The wooden fence on running board could hold luggage and there was a large "boot" in the rear. Locomobiles were made in Bridgeport, Connecticut. *Oregon Historical Society*

The Chicago Telephone Company used this circa-1920 Pierce-Arrow for carrying employees. Located in Buffalo, Pierce-Arrow was known best for its high-quality automobiles. *Illinois Bell Telephone*

A Giant bus body on a circa-1920 Samson. *Giant Manufacturing Co.*

Dalton's Bus Lines of Chickamauga, Georgia, used this 1920 White. The bus carried 35 passengers. Pneumatic tires gave a smoother ride and allowed higher operating speeds. *Volvo/White*

CHAPTER THREE

1921-1930

The July 15, 1922, issue of *The Commercial Vehicle* described two buses mounted on White truck chassis and purchased by Chicago's posh Edgewater Beach Hotel:

The coach builders who made the bodies were given *carte blanche* to provide a body that should be as luxurious as could be built. The interior is arranged in three seat sections, four passengers to a seat and all of them facing forward. Entrance is through limousine doors on the right side of the bus. In addition, the buses have upper decks, reached from the rear, which carry three double seats and three single seats. The upholstery of the interior is done in gray mohair plush. The backs of the seats are fastened to a movable anchorage, which provides just enough "give" in going over rough pavements, to absorb the jolts and shocks usually experienced by heavy vehicles. A winding staircase at the rear gives access to the upper deck. Brass handrails are provided. A deck screen surmounted with a heavy brass rail encircles the top. Electric green is the predominating color. The wheels are of primrose yellow, while primrose striping and black fenders complete the color scheme. The hotel crest decorates the lower panel of the central door.

The Fageol Safety Coach, introduced in 1921 or 1922 for intercity service, is generally credited as being

This unique rig was used in Skagway, Alaska. The right side of the body was carried forward to enclose an area above the hood. Passengers sat on a single seat, above the hood, facing the vehicle's left. Skagway is north of Juneau and adjacent to British Columbia. It was a boomtown at the beginning of this century because of the Klondike gold rush. *Glenbow, Alberta Institute*

the first vehicle designed specifically as a bus. The Fageol Safety Coach was undoubtedly the most significant bus of this era. It had a low center of gravity and was powered by a Hall Scott engine. In 1923, models were introduced that had air suspension in all four corners.

The 1920s was the era when the intercity bus industry began. Albert E. Meier and John P. Hoschek, in *Over the Road: A History of Intercity Bus Transportation in the United States*, wrote:

It was in the newest territories that the railroads were the least well developed and the most vulnerable to the rise of new competition. In the timber country of the Pacific Northwest, the iron and copper ranges of Minnesota, the oil fields of Texas, and especially the rich agricultural lands of California, population and commerce were growing faster than railroads could follow. Here the tiny seeds first sprouted. Here an industry was born.

Firestone wrote that in 1925, there were more than 6,500 bus companies in the United States, operating on 7,800 routes. This was slightly over one route per company, which tells us much of how the intercity industry originated. In 1928, the first coast-to-coast bus service was introduced.

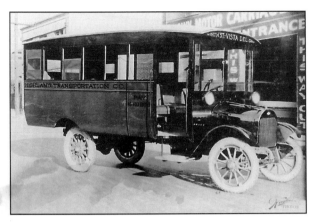

An early 1920s Chevrolet with a Crown body. *Crown Coach Corp.*

The name Fred Harvey is associated with railroad dining cars and with opening up Arizona and New Mexico to tourists. In 1925, Harvey's firm announced its program of "Indian Detours." Tourists would leave Santa Fe trains in either Albuquerque or Las Vegas (New Mexico) and travel by bus to the other, via Santa Fe. The "Detours" took three days with two nights spent in Harvey hotels. The third night, the traveler (referred to as a "Detourist") would be continuing on a train with Pullman sleeping car equipment. The tours expanded, and 28 different excursions were advertised in 1929, including some that toured the Grand Canyon. Archival photographs of equipment show Yellow and White buses used as "Harveycoaches." Large Packards were used as "Harveycars." And a 1928 Packard automobile advertisement said, "It is natural that the Santa Fe, famous for the perfection of its service and equipment, should provide Packard Eight cars exclusively for these deluxe explorations by those who demand the acme of comfort and luxury in transportation—either by rail or motor."

Some White trucks were employed to carry luggage only. According to D. H. Thomas in *The Southwestern Indian Detours*, in 1930 the Santa Fe firm had General Motors design a half-open brougham-style bus for its exclusive use, but no orders were ever placed, probably due to the Depression. The "Detours" declined steadily during the 1930s both because of the Depression and the fact that an increasing number of tourists now owned their own automobiles.

In 1925, Mack published a book for bus properties entitled *Bus Operating Practice*. Some of its chapter titles included: "Growth of the bus industry"; "Selecting profitable bus routes"; "Securing the right to run"; "Passenger terminals and waiting rooms"; "Selling the service"; "Operation"; "Indirect and supplementary revenue"; "Costs"; and "Selection of equipment." The "Selection of equipment" chapter was particularly helpful to bus operating companies, as it discussed such matters as price comparisons, judging the maker for quality and service, choosing manufactured or assembled buses, the drawbacks of assembled units, considerations for the driver, and servicing assembled buses. This chapter also discussed the actual construction of the buses, including ruggedness, economy, frame construction, riding qualities, the engine, vibration and balance, the transmission, the rear axle, final drive, brakes, brake adjustment, and body construction.

Mack's sales of buses for use on rail tracks during this decade were the highest. Principal customers were railroads, who were trying to cut their expenses on lightly used passenger lines. Railroads also used highway buses for the same purpose, as well as for carrying passengers to and from rail stations still served by train. By 1928, buses had replaced rail passenger service on 3,850 miles of track.

In cities, streetcar tracks were, by their very nature, inflexible. Streetcars could only drop passengers off and pick them up at the tracks. Buses were used to provide more widespread service. In 1929, the city of Knoxville, Tennessee, introduced its first five buses, to extend service beyond the streetcar tracks.

Motor Coach Age magazine contains articles about various bus properties (operations) and usually includes an equipment roster telling when equipment was purchased. It's difficult to follow most rosters exactly because of leased equipment, equipment lost to accidents, and equipment traded, permanently or temporarily.

The first motor bus was adopted into the Utica, New York, system in 1921 when the street railway operator took over the operation of a bus route that connected with a town about 10 miles away. The adopted vehicle was a 1912 Mack with a 26-seat Brill body. The street railway operator then created two bus subsidiaries, one with six Brockways with Kuhlman bodies, and the other with six Brockway trackless trolleys (electric powered with rubber tires, and connected to overhead wiring). During the balance of the decade, about nine White buses and three Macks were added to the fleet. All were gasoline powered and some were involved in what might be called "suburban" or "intercity" service.

The January 1980 issue of *Motor Coach Age* contained an article about Monterey Peninsula Transit and its predecessor, Bay Rapid Transit, a private operator. The Monterey area offered several opportunities for charters and tours. During the 1920s, Bay Rapid Transit's roster consisted of four Fords, three REOs, two Whites, and one each A.C.F., Fageol, and Yellow.

Meier and Hoschek reported statistics on intercity buses for the half century stretching from 1925 to 1975. In 1926, there were 4,040 companies, operating 22,800 buses, carrying 187 million revenue passengers. By 1930, the number of revenue passengers increased to 310 million, while the number of firms had dropped to

This photo, taken in Sand Point, Idaho, in the early 1920s, shows a Ford school bus, which was the first school bus used in nearby Sagle. On the side of the hood is metal framework, the size of a small crib, holding stretched canvas. Its purpose is unknown, although a guess would be that it formed a temporary seat. *Chuck Peterson*

3,520 and the number of buses to 14,090. These drops are evidence of consolidation and larger equipment.

According to a recent article in *School Bus Fleet*, during the 1927–1928 school year, only 12 percent of the school transportation vehicles used in 32 states surveyed still were horse-drawn. The motorized school bus was to have a great impact on rural America, because it made the one-room school extinct. Students would be bused to a larger school where, presumably, the education was better because teachers could specialize. However, the loss of the one-room school hurt many hamlets, where the school had been the community focal point. This was one factor involved in the decline of rural America. According to Albert C. Rose's *Historic American Roads*, in 1918 the United States had over 196,000 one-room schools; by 1936 this number had dropped to 131,000.

A. J. Brosseau, president of Mack Trucks, in a 1927 talk to the Bus Division of the American Automobile Association, noted:

If we glance at the statistics of bus use, we will find that of the 80,000 vehicles now in service, 32,778 are employed in transporting children back and forth from school. But let me point out that for future bus use here is one of the largest fields. The child of today is the citizen of tomorrow. The bus is not only making it possible for him to go to better schools, but he is becoming accustomed to that vehicle as a means of transportation.

In A. G. McMillan's *Model A/AA Ford Truck Owner* reprints of sales materials distributed to Ford dealers circa 1930, there was a booklet given to Ford Truck salesmen to help with sales. Included were ads from several bus body manufacturers. One firm, the FitzJohn Manufacturing Company of Muskegon, Michigan, advertised a 21-passenger bus for short hauls and feeder lines, to be placed on a Ford AA 157-inch wheelbase chassis. It was constructed of hardwood framework with metal bracing. The roof was oil duck, and body panels were sheet steel. The floor was linoleum. It had three dome lights, roof ventilators, and a hot air heater. The front door was folding and an emergency exit opened on

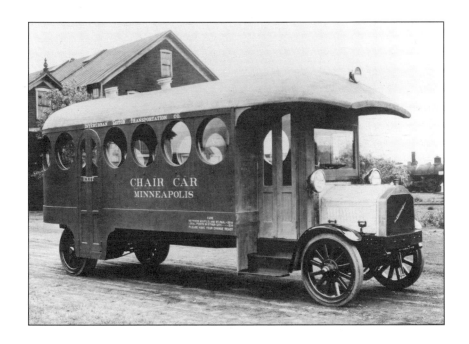

This circa-1920 United chassis with an enclosed bus body operated in the Minneapolis-St. Paul area. Fares listed on side are 20 cents between Minneapolis and St. Paul, and 10 cents for local stops in either city. Note the exit door is in the rear. *Railway Negative Exchange*

Fageols were built in Oakland, although in the mid-1920s their buses were made in Kent, Ohio. This early 1920s Fageol double-decker was used for sightseeing in southern Florida. Note that the top is open, although covered, while the bottom is enclosed. *Florida Photographic Archives*

These three Ford school buses on extended frames from the early 1920s were used in California. *Fabco*

the left side toward the rear. The body price was $1,750, F.O.B. Muskegon. Accessories were also listed including a roof luggage rack for $40 and shatterproof glass, $112 for the entire body.

United Automotive Body Co. of Springboro, Pennsylvania, built 12-foot and 14-foot school bus bodies with the body mounted on a REO chassis. Under "method of shipment" in the specifications was this statement:

> United School Bodies shipped either KD [knocked down] or crated set up, or where three set-up bodies can be shipped in one [rail] car, crating is not necessary. With many of the truck plants United has an arrangement whereby United School bodies are kept in stock and the complete job—chassis and body—is shipped to the dealer from the factory, thus saving the freight on the bodies.

One change in buses that occurred late in the decade was the adoption of the "street car" shape. The entire body was made rectangular with the engine placed either underneath or in the rear. Most urban and intercity buses soon adopted this shape. School buses were the slowest to change. Some intercity buses adopted the "deck and a half design," with the rear portion of the bus at a higher level and a windshield for the passengers to view the scenery. In the mid-1920s, Greyhound established its package express service, and soon separate compartments were provided for carrying freight and parcels.

The American Public Transit Association (APTA) estimates that by 1930, local transit buses were boarding about 2.5 billion passengers annually. APTA also indicated that in 1923 three cities, Bay City, Michigan, Everett, Washington, and Newburgh, New York, eliminated all their streetcars, replacing them with buses.

Wren and Wren noted that this was the decade when double-decked buses were introduced on Fifth Avenue in New York City. The year was 1922, and the bus operator had to purchase snowplows to mount on the front in order to keep the bus routes open. In the same year, some buses operating between Oakland and Sacramento were equipped with radios for the listening enjoyment of passengers. Some multidoor buses had a master door lock which allowed the driver to lock or unlock all doors from the driver's seat. Other bus features appearing in this decade were pull cords, allowing passengers to request a stop; air brakes and air-operated doors; individual reading lights; and ash trays. By 1927, 82 percent of the buses had six-cylinder engines; 73 percent had four-speed transmissions, and 88 percent had pneumatic tires.

This was also the decade when the "Good Roads" movement became active. Bus companies lobbied for paved, maintained roads between cities, important to the development of bus operations. One industry problem developing was the conflict between different state laws specifying bus dimensions and safety equipment. In addition to making it difficult for a manufacturer to achieve economies of scale enjoyed by mass producing, the conflicting rules made it difficult to operate buses on routes that connected two or more states.

A 1922 Kissel, built in Hartford, Wisconsin. The sign at rear of the rooftop luggage rack says: "The Boulevard." The printing on the photo says this is a "Kissel DeLuxe Coach Limited." *The William F. Harrah Automobile Foundation*

Seldens were built in Rochester, New York, although the Selden name is known best because of the Selden patent which, it was claimed, covered the automobile. This is a 1922 Selden demonstrator. Lettered on the side are the words: "Selden Motorbus." *National Automotive History Collection, Detroit Public Library*

This is an open tour bus used in Vancouver, B.C. The tour guide's seat is on the front fender facing the passengers. He used a megaphone. Passengers are seated four abreast. *Vancouver Public Library*

Passengers on this 1922 White make use of luggage racks on top of fenders. The bus is headed for San Bernardino. National Automotive History Collection, Detroit Public Library

Merrill Horine, writing in a 1925 issue of *The Automobile Trimmer and Painter*, said:

In a recent enacted Massachusetts law, for example, a gearshift diagram is required. The writer knows of only one standard bus deviating from the S.A.E. standard on gearshift positions. Wisconsin prohibits the use of double-decked buses in interurban service. On its face this sounds like a joke, but are we sure that provision will not definitely bar out the new observation type buses which have recently appeared on the Pacific Coast, wherein the after part of the body is raised about three feet higher than the front part, providing a baggage space beneath and improving the view for the passengers behind.

Bus operators were familiar with requirements for continual maintenance and the problems associated by breakdowns while buses were on the road. The 1932 book *Making Bus Operations Pay* discussed the 1930 records for motor buses operated on seven routes by the Detroit Department of Street Railways, listing the cause of 712 road delays. The major problems and their frequency include: engine, 175; tires, 140; ignition, 75; accelerator, 43; transmission and clutch, 37; gas line, 33; axle, 29; battery, 28; brakes, 24; carburetor and vacuum, 23; starter and generator, 19; cooling system 17; fan assembly, 14; out of gas, 14; and wheels, 12. The book also gave an "on the road" tire failure record for an unspecified bus property for the year 1929. This was compared with the bus miles operated by that property each month. July was the toughest month on tires, with on the road tire repair needed every 14,400 bus miles; November was the best with a tire repair every 125,600 bus miles.

The book also contained the results of a survey of bus properties regarding light bulb life. The Toronto Transportation Commission reported that headlight bulbs averaged 4,022 miles; body light bulbs, 20,403 miles; and marker and taillight bulbs, 14,119 miles. The Cincinnati Street Railway reported 2,406 miles per bulb in head lamps; 1,177 miles per bulb in markers, taillamps, and auxiliary outside lamps; and 1,810 miles per bulb from inside lamps. The Roanoke Railway & Electric Company reported that head lamp bulbs gave 2,941 miles of service; marker and taillamps 5,172 miles; and inside lamps 1,923 miles.

Previous Page
This open White bus had two more horsepower added to help it through the snow in Rocky Mountain National Park. The man standing on the spare tire must not expect the bus to be moving soon. The photo was taken in 1923. *Rocky Mountain National Park*

In the mid-1920s, Yellowstone had a fleet of 279 White buses, and was one of the largest bus fleets in the nation. This 1922 White "national park bus" operated in Yellowstone. At one time this bus was at the Van Horn Truck Museum in Mason City, Iowa. *Lloyd Van Horn*

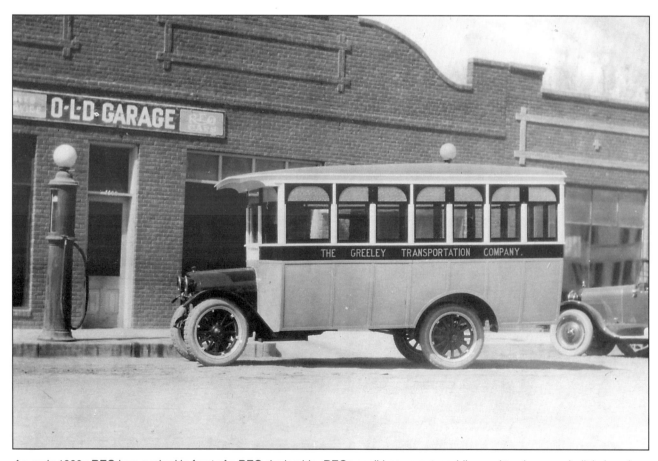

An early 1920s REO bus, parked in front of a REO dealership. REOs, well-known automobiles and trucks, were built in Lansing, Michigan. *National Tour Association*

This Charabanc enclosed bus body on a chassis built by U.S. Truck was built, and used, in the Cincinnati area. *National Automotive History Collection, Detroit Public Library*

Originally a "hunt" vehicle, this early 1920s White was used by the Hollywood Golf and Country Club in Florida to carry guests to and from the links. It has two levels, with a stairway in back, and holders for the golf clubs. On the side of the door is a monogram. The photo was taken in 1926. *Florida Photographic Archives, Strozier Library, Florida State University*

The Orange Blossom Stage Line used this early 1920s White. Two front compartments were labeled "LADIES," and a window separated them from the "SMOKING" compartment in the rear. Luggage space was inside, behind the rear seat. The sign under the rear window says: "Heated-Insured Carrier." New Haven Carriage & Auto Works, Portland, Oregon

The Youngstown & Suburban Transportation Co. used this 1923 White "chair car." The interior view faces forward and shows wicker seating. National Automotive History Collection, Detroit Public Library

This Yuba crawler tractor pulled several wagonloads of tourists on Catalina Island in California in the early 1920s. California State Library

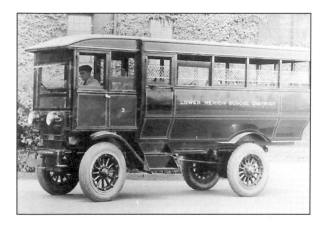

A 1924 Autocar with a school bus body. Free Library of Philadelphia

A 1924 Fageol used as an urban bus. The William F. Harrah Automobile Foundation

This 1924 Federal open bus had side curtains. National Automotive History Collection, Detroit Public Library

Note the temporary side curtain on the mid-1920s White. This bus operated between Corinth and Saratoga, New York. The tires on the front are pneumatic, and those in the rear are solid. Kelly-Springfield

Bender bodies were built in Cleveland. This Bender body is on an unknown chassis, circa 1925. *Free Library of Philadelphia*

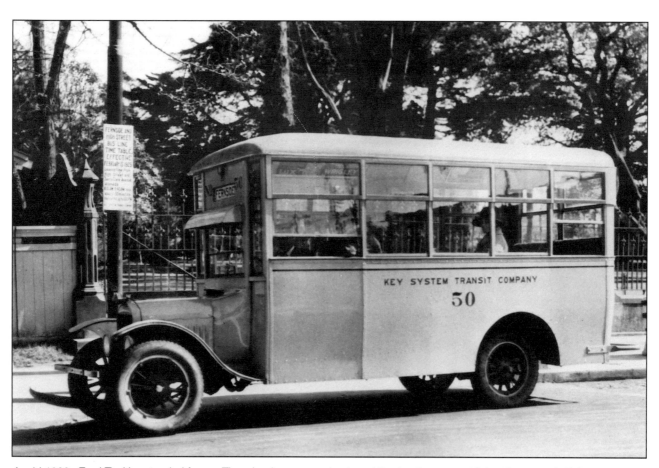

A mid-1920s Ford T with extended frame. The wheels are oversized, and the fenders seem higher than usual. *Fabco*

This 1925 Graham Bros. chassis bus was used in Pennsylvania. Note the rear end. The wording on the door says: "C. N. Dicks Auto Bus, P.S.C.C. NO. A 9240." The letters probably stand for Pennsylvania State Commerce Commission and the number is of its permit or certificate to operate. At this time, Graham Bros. was closely associated with Dodge. *Smithsonian Institution*

A 1925 Graham Bros. school bus used in Gresham, Oregon. *Oregon Historical Society*

This mid-1920s International chassis had an intercity "parlor car" body built by Superior. Note that it has two doors on this side. *Superior Coach Division, Sheller Globe Corporation*

An interior view of a Giant school bus body on an International chassis, circa 1925. The bus loaded from the rear, and the seats were parallel to the bus. Giant Manufacturing Co.

The G. C. Kuhlman Car Co. of Cleveland built this bus. Wording on the side of the hood says: "Imperial Omnibus." The words painted on the side of the bus say: "Trackless Transportation Corporation, New York." Riveting is obvious. Smithsonian Institution

The Cincinnati Motor Bus Co. used this 1925 Schacht "Superior Safety Bus." The fancy headlights were called "Woodlights." Schachts were built in Cincinnati. National Automotive History Collection, Detroit Public Library

A mid-1920s Studebaker, used in Missouri. The operator was Garrison and Dalton of Doniphan. The rig has running lights and a large rear luggage carrier. State Historical Society of Missouri

The "Syracuse Railways Coordinated Bus Lines Inc." operated this fleet of mid-1920s Brockways. Brockway trucks were built in Cortland, New York, until 1977. University of Michigan

A 1926 Fageol Safety Coach. The William F. Harrah Automobile Foundation

A mid-1920s double-decked GM model Z used by the Chicago Motor Coach Co. The William F. Harrah Automobile Foundation

This mid-1920s Lincoln was operated by the Lincoln Limousine Line. The visor lists Los Angeles, Las Vegas, Salt Lake City, and Denver. This may be a conventional large auto. Note the spotlight, tool chest, and five-gallon Pennzoil dispenser strapped inside the spare—an indicator of oil consumption at that time. *Whittington Collection, CSU Long Beach*

A combined freight and passenger body was built by Proctor-Keefe and placed on a 1926 Republic chassis for service between De Tour and Sault Ste. Marie, in Upper Michigan. Proctor-Keefe truck and bus bodies were built in Detroit. *National Automotive History Collection, Detroit Public Library*

This is a circa-1926 Studebaker motor coach body. It is carrying a mobile broadcasting device and has an antenna strung between the two high poles. *The William F. Harrah Automobile Foundation*

This late 1920s A.C.F. parlor car had an observation deck. This design provided an enclosed luggage area below the raised deck. This bus was operated by a subsidiary of the New Haven Railroad, Motor Coach of New England Transportation Co. The railroad hoped to substitute bus for rail passenger service in unprofitable markets. By 1928, it was running 250 buses. This bus ran between New York and Boston and seated 29 passengers. A.C.F. was short for American Car & Foundry Co., located in Philadelphia. *Baker Library, Harvard University*

A 1927 Mack AL operating between Spring Valley and New York City. Its New York City terminal was the Hotel Knickerbocker. *National Automotive History Collection, Detroit Public Library*

The city bus body on this late 1920s Pierce-Arrow "Z" chassis was built by the Brown Body Corporation. The lettering on the side says: "Boise Street Car Company." Smithsonian Institution

Safeway buses were built by the Six-Wheel Co. of Philadelphia. This one was apparently used in northern Ohio. B. F. Goodrich Collection, Univ. of Akron Archives

This bus operating between Richmond, Virginia, and Washington, D.C., had to be pulled out of the mud by a crawler tractor. Virginia Department of Highways and Transportation

This Safeway bus was used in Damascus, Syria, and is shown posing for a Firestone tire ad. Firestone Archives

A late 1920s White bus on the crowded main street of a small town in Utah. Utah State Historical Society

Pictured in front of the train station at Charleston, South Carolina, is this circa-1927 White. *The Family Lines Rail System*

Greyhound, which originated in Minnesota, took over the Wilcox truck factory in Minneapolis in 1927 and used it to build buses until about 1930. The buses' make was "Will." This one, operated by Pacific Greyhound, is bogged down in the snow in northern Nevada, on its way to Salt Lake City. *Northeastern Nevada Museum, Elko*

This 1927 Yellow highway bus was used by the Naval Academy at Annapolis. The luggage compartment is on roof at rear. *American Automobile Manufacturers Assn.*

A pair of 1928 Federal buses used by Western State Teachers' College (now Western Michigan University). Note the scallop vent pattern on the top of the hood, usually associated with Fageols. *Western Michigan University Archives & Regional History Collections*

A fleet of GMC tour buses. The one on left has a blanket-like device to speed up engine heating in cold weather. It also has three license plates on the front bumper (apparently to allow operation in several states). The plate on the right is from New Hampshire, 1928. *National Tour Association*

A highway bus body on a 1928 Kenworth chassis. *Paccar*

A bus body under construction, carried on a late 1920s Studebaker chassis. *The William F. Harrah Automobile Foundation*

Right
American-LaFrance was the nation's premier fire apparatus builder for much of this century. For a brief period the company built commercial trucks. This is from one of its brochures showing bus bodies. *Free Library of Philadelphia*

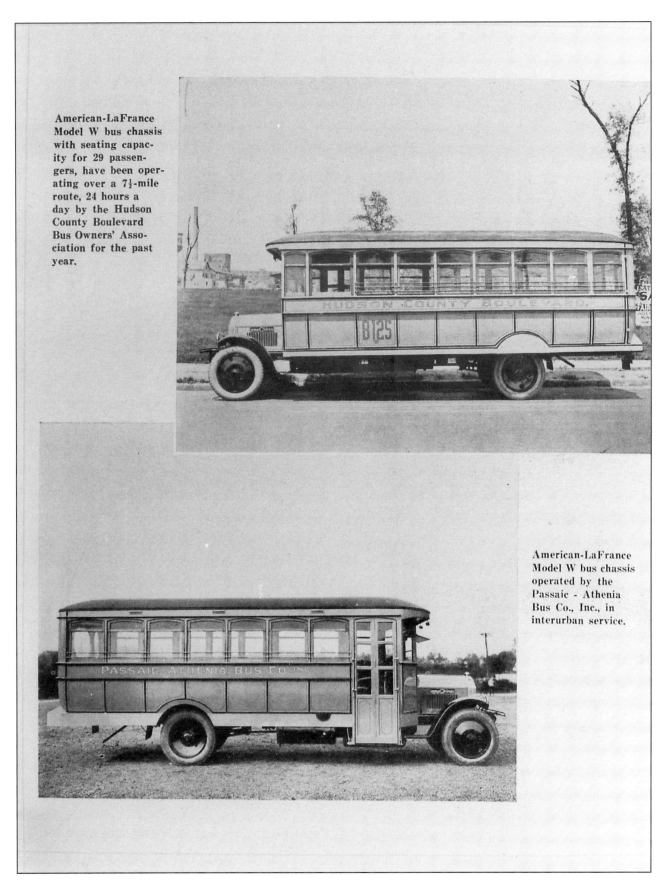

American-LaFrance Model W bus chassis with seating capacity for 29 passengers, have been operating over a 7½-mile route, 24 hours a day by the Hudson County Boulevard Bus Owners' Association for the past year.

American-LaFrance Model W bus chassis operated by the Passaic - Athenia Bus Co., Inc., in interurban service.

A Model AA Ford used as a bus in Oakland, California. *Railway Negative Exchange*

A small number of Pickwick "sleeper" coaches were built during the period 1928-1933, mainly for operations along the West Coast. There were 13 compartments, and each could accommodate two people. Seats could be converted into bunks for night-time travel. There was also a small galley and two lavatories. A steward would prepare and serve the meals. The builder was Pickwick Motor Coach Works of Los Angeles. The vehicle was powered by a 150-horsepower Sterling engine, which could be removed on tracks leading to the front. *Railway Negative Exchange*

For a short period around 1930, large automobile coupes became tractors by the addition of a fifth wheel device. This 1929 Studebaker pulls the equivalent of an airline limousine for Transcontinental Air Transport, a predecessor of TWA. The plane is a Ford Tri-Motor. *Trans World Airlines*

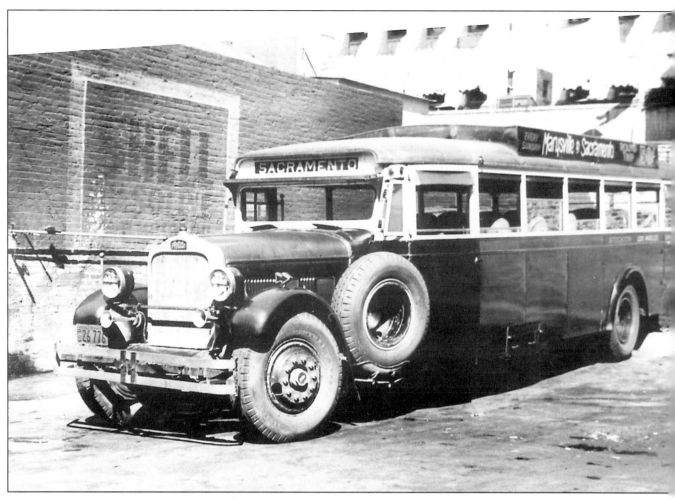

A 1929 White headed for Sacramento. *California State Archives*

A 21-passenger Yellow bus used by the Gary Street Railway. Note that the body barely extends beyond the rear axle. *Smithsonian Institution*

A circa-1930 Chevrolet with a Crown school bus body. Note the covered luggage rack at the rear. *Crown Coach Corp.*

A Ford AA with a crew bus body, used for servicing, tethering, and towing a Goodyear blimp. Outrider wheels add stability. *Goodyear Archives*

Copying an idea from railroad presidents who had their own "private" rail cars, Greyhound outfitted this coach for use by its top officials. The seating area could be converted into beds. *University of Michigan*

A 1930 International outfitted to operate on rail tracks near Santa Cruz, California. *Blackhawk Classic Auto Collection*

A circa-1930 double-decked Yellow Coach, used in the Baltimore area. *Smithsonian Institution*

A Yellow full-size bus pulling a full trailer. *Pullman-Trailmobile*

CHAPTER FOUR

1931-1940

The National Automobile Chamber of Commerce reported that there were 98,900 buses in the United States in 1931. This included 14,050 city buses; 22,750 intrastate intercity buses; 5,600 interstate intercity buses; 51,500 school buses; 3,000 sightseeing buses; 900 industrial buses, 700 hotel buses; and 400 miscellaneous buses.

This is the decade when many bus operations became subject to economic regulation. Railroads had been regulated in the late 1800s, after abusing their powers in markets by maintaining monopolies. However, economic regulations for highway carriers of freight and passengers were slower to develop. During this time, railroads lobbied for the regulations of trucks and buses because they were taking the most lucrative traffic, leaving the railroads with

This picture appeared in a brochure from the Mifflinsburg Body Co. of Mifflinsburg, Pennsylvania, showing its school bus body on a 1931 Chevrolet chassis. Seats were benches on each side of the truck bed. *Blackhawk Classic Auto Collection*

traffic they didn't want. (Railroads were common carriers and had a duty to serve all traffic and all customers.) The other group in favor of the regulation of buses was the bus passengers themselves, who wanted a more stable supply of service. Most bus operators also wanted some regulation, especially to protect themselves from "jitneys" who were taking away business from bus operators. Bus operators thought that a regulated market would be more orderly and more conducive to long-term investment in coaches.

Safety regulations, another item of concern, were enacted at first on the state level and then the federal level. As interstate travel progressed, the bus industry had to make sure that state regulations were reasonably similar in order for a vehicle to run in several states.

Also relevant was the ownership of the buses. School buses and local transit buses in a few large cities were publicly owned, and were usually subject only to safety regulations. Buses in private ownership, on the other hand, were usually subject to economic regulation as well as safety.

For regulatory purposes, highway carriers were placed into three categories, based on their relationship to users. "Private" carriers were those who charged no fares and carried either their own employees or patrons of their major enterprise, such as a hotel or resort bus. "Contract" carriers were leased for a single trip or for a period of time. For example, a visiting convention might charter buses to carry convention participants to a golf course. "Common" carriers were those who operated in a specified area, on a schedule, charged fares, and carried all passengers.

Common carriers sought an operating permit, usually called a "certificate of public convenience and necessity." This made them a common carrier with an obligation to carry safely all passengers, without discrimination, within their service area and at reasonable rates. A state or federal regulatory body was the ultimate judge of reasonable rates and service. For assuming these obligations, the common carrier received considerable protection from direct competitors. In some areas there would be no competitors, while in markets between major cities there might be two or three. Major carriers had elaborate systems of internal subsidies so that their more lucrative markets could subsidize those markets that could not cover full costs. Note that the regulatory system offered the buses no protection from competition from automobiles or airlines.

Most common carrier firms got to keep whatever routes they were operating on in 1935. These routes, or "operating authorities," were said to be "grandfathered." The rights to these routes could be bought and sold so that they could be connected into a larger system; that was one way that Greyhound and others would expand.

This economic regulatory system stayed in place at the federal level until 1982. State economic regulation ended in the 1990s. State regulation of urban bus systems became moot by about 1970, by which time most private systems had been taken over by local governments.

During this entire period, Greyhound was expanding into nationwide service. It did this by acquiring some firms and entering into traffic interchange agreements with others. Greyhound would become the nation's primary intercity highway passenger carrier.

Buses were beginning to eat away at railroad traffic. A 1932 report of the Interstate Commerce Commission said, in part:

> Experience to date indicates that the field of passenger transportation has been divided between bus and steam railroad carriers about as follows: On local, main and branch lines buses and the private car have almost completely superseded rail service; for moderate distances up to about 150 miles, bus service has strong competitive powers, even where rail service is frequent and otherwise adequate to the public's requirements; for intermediate distances up to about 250 miles the marked difference in elapsed time en route and in comforts is only partially overcome by lower bus charges and possibly greater convenience of schedules and points of arrival and departure, and in this field the railroad has an advantage; for long distances, rail service is so decidedly superior to bus service for most travelers that even substantially lower bus fares do not create a large volume of traffic. (Source: Docket No. 23400, 1932, page 374, cited in *Taxation of Motor Vehicle Transportation.* New York: National Industrial Conference Board, 1932, p. 151.)

In the airlines, a related passenger industry, a very significant development occurred in 1935 with the introduction of the Douglas DC-3. This airplane became the standard building block for the nation's (and much of the world's) airline industry. It was as sig-

A 1931 Fageol operated by the Market Street Railway Co. in San Francisco. *Smithsonian Institution*

nificant to airways as was the Ford Model T to highway transportation. Its significance to the bus industry was that air travel would prove to be a formidable competitor in many intercity markets. While more costly, it was much faster.

In 1937, North Carolina became the first state to have an organized training program for school bus drivers. In 1939, the first national conference was held that dealt with construction standards for school buses, and the "school bus yellow" color was adopted. A total of 44 school bus standards established at the conference helped the bus manufacturers, as they could now build more standardized models. School buses were being built in many sizes. Dodge school bus chassis for 1940 included the 1 1/2-ton chassis with wheelbase lengths of 133, 160, and 190 inches; and the 2-ton chassis with lengths of 136, 160, 178, and 220 inches.

By now, a number of truck manufacturers were providing longer chassis for school bus bodies. These long chassis found a second use, as fire department ladder trucks. During the Depression, many cash-strapped fire departments built ladder trucks on a bus chassis in their own shops.

Suppliers of truck and bus bodies advertised in catalogs, printed each year for dealers of each major make of truck. *The Silver Book*, distributed to Chevrolet dealers,

The engine cculd be pulled forward for maintenance on this 1931 Fageol. *Security Pacific National Bank, Historical Collection*

This 1931 White was one of eight delivered to the Yellowstone Park Transportation Co., a concession operator at Yellowstone National Park. It had a canvas roof, which is shown open, allowing passengers to stand. Six stays across the top joined the sides. To open the roof, the canvas was rolled rearward. The vehicle weighed five tons and cost $8,000. *Volvo/White*

contained about 200 pages of ads for bodies and equipment that could be installed on a chassis. The chassis would be shipped first to the body builder, then to the dealer for delivery. Similar books were prepared for dealers of other truck makes as well. In the 1938 *Silver Book* were ads for school buses built by Blue Bird Body Company of Fort Valley, Georgia; Bender Body Company of Cleveland; and Hicks Body Company of Lebanon, Indiana. Two other bus builders with ads were FitzJohn, which advertised both urban bus and stretched auto bodies, and Wickett Motor Service Corp. of Richmond, Indiana (associated with the Wayne Corporation), which built forward control buses on Chevrolet chassis.

Developments of the decade reported by Wren and Wren include the crossing of the continent in 1932 by a Mack bus equipped with a Cummins diesel engine. *Motor* magazine, in May 1937, reported that White had experimented with air conditioning in a bus. Tests, conducted in Texas, used Kelvinator cooling equipment, powered by a small gasoline engine located in a rear compartment.

During this decade, the street railroad in Utica, New York, added to its fleet of buses. It received 33 Twin Coaches, 5 A.C.F.s, 7 Macks, 3 Whites, 1 Yellow, and 1 Ford. Some of this equipment was used to replace streetcar operations. On the West Coast, in Monterey, California, Bay Rapid Transit added six Whites (three

This is a Mack, from the early 1930s. The lettering on the side says "Cummins Diesel Engine Test Bus Coast to Coast." This took place in 1932. *Western Highway Institute*

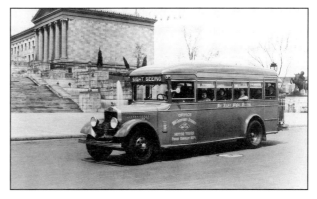

Gray Lines Tours used this 1932 White. *Smithsonian Institution*

that carried 40 passengers, and three that carried 21 passengers) and one Flxible.

APTA estimates that by 1940, the first year that bus ridership exceeded streetcar ridership, local transit buses were boarding about 4.3 billion passengers annually.

In the late 1930s, the National City Lines, whose principal owners included General Motors, Mack, Firestone Tire & Rubber, Phillips Petroleum, and Standard Oil Company of California, aggressively took over street railroads in a number of major cities, replacing streetcars with buses.

Meier and Hoschek reports for 1940 show that the intercity bus industry had lost ground over the decade. In 1940, there were 1,830 companies, operating 12,200 buses, carrying 238 million revenue passengers. It can be assumed that the drop-off is due mainly to the automobile.

The 1930s are probably the most interesting decade in the development of autos, trucks, and buses. By the decade's end, the vehicles in use were modern and could be operated today. The most significant bus appeared late in the decade. It was the Greyhound Silversides bus, designed by Raymond Loewy and built by General Motors. About 500 were built before World War II and about 2,000 in 1947 and 1948. During World War II, when more people became dependent on bus transportation, the Greyhound Silversides offered one of the only methods of intercity travel. In the movies, when young men were shown leaving their hometown to go off to war, they were often shown boarding a Greyhound Silversides.

This 1933-34 Ford tractor/semitrailer had the driver sitting in the trailer, allowing him access to passengers and vice-versa. Note the curtains in windows. The body was built by Wentworth and Irwin of Portland, Oregon, and apparently was operated in Washington State. *Columbia Body & Equipment Co.*

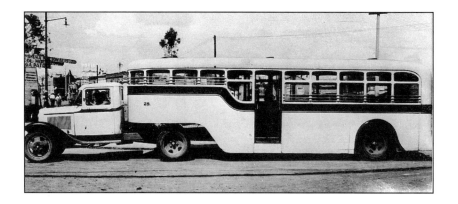

This Fruehauf semitrailer bus was pulled by an early 1933-34 Ford V-8. The signs in left of picture are in Spanish. Fruehauf trailers were made in Detroit. *American Truck Historical Society*

This early 1930s A.C.F. was used by the Santa Fe railroad to connect with rail trains. It had double jack-knife doors on each side of the front, allowing passengers to unload quickly at the station so they could reach their trains. *Institute of Transportation Studies, University of California*

All American Bus Lines operated this Crown sleeper coach, built in the mid-1930s. This one was named "Miss California." *Crown Coach Corp.*

A three-quarters view of a 1933 Indiana city coach. *Volvo/White*

A 1933 Indiana, used in Cleveland. In 1932, White acquired the Indiana Motors Corporation. *Volvo/White*

This 1933 International carried a bus body with "ahead of its time" windshield streamlining. It was used at Chicago's Century of Progress. *Navistar Archives*

A mid-1930s A.C.F. with a "deck and a half" body installed by Wentworth and Irwin in Portland, Oregon. This one was operated by North Coast Lines. Columbia Body & Equipment Co.

A 1934 Federal with a Hackney body used by a German Protestant Orphans' Home. National Automotive History Collection, Detroit Public Library

Wentworth and Irwin of Portland, Oregon, built this 25-passenger bus for Mt. Hood Stages in the mid-1930s. Columbia Body & Equipment Co.

This is a 1935 stretched Chevrolet, parked in front of the delivering dealership. Note the running lights and luggage rack. The two center doors on the driver's side did not open. The owner was Northland DeLuxe Lines. On the side is painted the names of some of the cities it serviced, including Chicago and Calumet. National Automotive History Collection, Detroit Public Library

A 1935 DeSoto Airflow used by the Mount Hood Stages. The roof rack could be reached by ladder on the trunk. Columbia Body & Equipment Co.

This is a combined bus and freight body that was used in rural areas, especially as railroad passenger service was abandoned. This Gillig body was placed on a 1935 Diamond-T chassis, and operated in northern California. Gillig started out in San Francisco in 1890 and in 1938 moved to Hayward, California, where it is still building buses. Gillig built its first school bus in 1932. Gillig Corp

This photo demonstrates the strength of a Gillig all-steel school bus body. The chassis is a 1935 Ford. Gillig Corp.

Gar Wood, a Detroit truck body builder, built this bus in 1935. The engine was rear-mounted. *National Automotive History Collection, Detroit Public Library*

These are Hackney bodies on a pair of 1935 GMC chassis, used between Burlington and Graham, North Carolina. The sign by the door says that the cash fare is 10 cents, and four tokens are a quarter. *Hackney Bros. Body Co.*

A 1935 Kenworth with a "deck and a half" passenger compartment. *Paccar*

North Coast Lines ran this 1935 Kenworth. *Paccar*

A 1935 Mack. Free Library of Philadelphia

In the 1930s, Mack built some over-sized trucks for use in heavy construction, such as the dams being built in the Southwest. This oversized Mack "work bus" has a double-deck bus body. Compare its size to the trailing International. In the picture, the Mack appears to be tilting toward the right. Library of Congress

Marmon-Herrington of Indianapolis built all-wheel-drive conversion packages for Ford trucks, as well as some large all-wheel-drive trucks, during the 1930s. Many of these products were exported for use in other countries. This Marmon-Herrington 10-wheel tractor pulls a bus semitrailer. This is one of two "Nairn" buses, operated on a 15-hour, 530-mile run over open desert between Damascus, Syria, and Baghdad, Iraq. The two units were built by Budd in 1935. American Automobile Manufacturers Assn.

A 1935 Pierce-Arrow, on a stretched chassis, used in Yosemite National Park. *Yosemite National Park*

This 1935 REO carried the Viking Accordion Band of Albert Lea, Minnesota. The emblem on the side of the hood says: "REO Safety Bus." *Freeborn County Historical Society, Albert Lea, MN*

A 1935 Twin Coach, built in Kent, Ohio. Note that the rear axles are at the end of the frame. *Smithsonian Institution*

When is the last time you saw a bus driver in boots like these? These drivers worked for the Key System, which operated in the San Francisco Bay area. The bus is a circa-1935 Twin Coach. *AC Transit*

Chicago Surface Lines used this 1935 White. The small letters near the rear door say "out," to indicate that passengers should board at the front door, where fares were collected. *Smithsonian Institution*

Three bathing beauties on the roof of a 1935 Yellow operated by the Santa Fe Trail System. This promotional photo was taken in San Francisco, with the newly completed Bay Bridge in the background. *University of Akron Archives*

This mid-1930s photos shows a fleet of school buses that served the high school in Santa Rosa, California. The two buses on the left are probably REOs; the three on the right are Fageols.

A small bus on a mid-1930s Ford chassis. The aluminum body was built in the shops of Detroit's Department of Street Railways, and was apparently a prototype. *Baker Library, Harvard University*

These trams—pulled by 1936 Fords—were used in the Golden Gate International Exposition, held in San Francisco in 1939. Later, they were used at San Francisco's zoo and, briefly, on the campus of San Francisco State College. *Baker Library, Harvard University*

A bus body on a semitrailer, built by Fruehauf. The tractor is a 1936 Ford. This rig was used for tours at Ford's River Rouge plant. *Union City Body Co*

A 1936 Indiana school bus used in Franklin, New York. *Volvo/White*

Gillig used a mid-1930s International chassis to carry this cab-forward school bus. There is an overhead luggage rack and ladder at the rear leading to it. Gillig Corp.

This Gillig body on a mid-1930s REO chassis had a destination sign reading "Fresno." In 1936, REO stopped building autos and concentrated on trucks and buses. Gillig Corp.

A small FitzJohn 22-passenger bus on a 1936 Studebaker chassis, used in Logansport. FitzJohn bodies were built in Muskegon, Michigan. The William F. Harrah Automobile Foundation

This 1936 White tractor pulled an excursion bus for the Great Lakes Exposition, held in Cleveland. Greyhound Lines sponsored this bus. Volvo/White

A 1937 A.C.F., operated by Santa Fe Trailways, an offshoot of the railroad. Institute of Transportation Studies, University of California

American Airlines owned these seven 1937 Chrysler Custom Imperial limousines. They have fender-mounted spares, and the trunks appear to be larger than those on conventional passenger models. *Baker Library, Harvard University*

A 1937-38 Dodge with a Superior school bus body. *Superior Coach Division, Sheller Globe Corporation*

A forward-mounted bus body was carried on a 1937 Ford chassis. The bus operated in the Russian River area, about 75 miles north of San Francisco. The sign on the front advertises Woody Herman's band. *Railway Negative Exchange*

Gillig used 1937 International chassis to build these two small buses for Vallejo, California. The paint pattern follows a "streamlined" concept of the 1930s. *Gillig Corp.*

This 1937 photo shows the Greyhound Bus terminal in Charleston, West Virginia. The bus at the right appears to be a GMC/Yellow Super Coach. Greyhound built terminals in many cities, in sites close to the central business district. Some of its "cut-rate" competitors had contractual relationships with hotels to use the hotel lobbies as their terminals. *National Automotive History Collection, Detroit Public Library*

A late 1930s White "national park" bus. Rich Nelson

A field full of 1938 Chevrolet bus chassis, outside the Hackney plant in Wilson, North Carolina. Hackney Bros. Body Co.

A late 1930s Flxible spotted at a "Bus Bash" in Portland, Oregon, a few years ago. Flxible was founded in 1912, initially to manufacture motorcycle sidecars. Flxible buses were built in Loudonville, Ohio, until 1974 when the firm moved to Delaware, Ohio, where it exists today. The spelling of the name—which must drive all proofreaders and spell checkers crazy —dates to 1919, when that particular spelling was needed so that the company could copyright it.

The people in Superior, Wisconsin, apparently felt that they needed an FWD to handle their winters. This one is from the late 1930s. FWD

A Hicks school bus body on a late 1930s International. The Hicks Body Company was located in Lebanon, Indiana. Navistar Archives

An open park bus on a 1938 Kenworth chassis. The Olivine Corp. of Seattle has restored one of these rigs.

A late 1930s Mack outfitted with bench seats, used to carry workers in Iran. *Mack Museum*

This 14-passenger stretched 1938 Packard Super-Eight, with roof rack and canvas-covered rear luggage rack, was used in California. A seascape mural is painted on the center door. The photo was initially filed as an exhibit in a California P.U.C. hearing and was labeled "proposed equipment." *California State Archives*

The Western State Teachers College of Kalamazoo used this 1938 REO. Note the fog lights and fancy paint job. Western Michigan University Archives and Regional History Collection

Mohawk Stages operated this late 1930s bus, built on a Studebaker chassis. *The William F. Harrah Automobile Foundation*

In 1939, American Airlines had a dozen 12-passenger Cadillac limousines built by Meteor Motor Company of Piqua, Ohio, for use at airports in New York, Chicago, and Detroit. The limousines' interior color scheme was the same as that inside American Airlines planes. The limos had roof racks. *National Automotive History Collection, Detroit Public Library*

A 1939 Chevrolet cab-over with a Gillig school bus body, for use in Madera, California. *Gillig Corp.*

Several Pennsylvania fire departments operated this sort of vehicle. Our guess is that it's a form of a crew bus; most of the volunteers would assemble at the station and ride in this bus, rather than drive individually to the fire site. The chassis is probably a late-1930s Diamond-T. The body builder was Schnabel, located in Pittsburgh. Historical Society of Western Pennsylvania

A long Gillig school bus body on a 1939 GMC chassis. GMC Corp.

This 1939 White was operated by Queen City Trailways and has a Hackney body. Hackney built school buses from 1920 until 1962. According to a company history, the firm built school bus bodies in the summer so they would be ready for the fall, and refrigerated bodies during the remainder of the year. As demand for refrigerated bodies grew, Hackney dropped school buses because they were less profitable to build. Hackney Bros. Body Co.

This 1940 photo shows the drawbacks of relying solely on rear exit doors. Note the turn indicator arrow. A long rod leads to the front, where the driver moves it manually. Gillig Corp.

CHAPTER FIVE

1941-1950

The bus industry played a significant role during World War II. Gasoline and tires for automobiles were rationed, so individuals often had to ride buses in place of their own automobiles. Secondly, new war plants and military bases were often located in newly developed areas that could be reached only by bus.

The national speed limit was set at 35 miles per hour, but the intercity bus industry complained that this speed was too low, as many buses had to go faster than that to be in "top" gear. The result of the low speed limit was continual shifting, which was hard on the transmission, engine, tires, and brake drums. The industry conducted tests using two pairs of eight buses each, one of which would travel at 35 miles per hour, the other at 40 miles per hour. "Each bus was equipped with new tires which had been carefully weighed on accurate scales before they were put on the wheels. At the conclusion of the test runs, the tires were removed and again weighed on the same scales. The results of these tests showed that actually 4.7 percent less rubber was consumed by those buses operated at 40 miles per hour than by those held down to 35 miles per hour," according to *Intercity Buses at War*.

Because of the war, new bus production was sharply curtailed, and the "nation's bus operators have rebuilt

The roof was raised on this 1941 Chevrolet panel truck to build this small bus. The work was done by Gillig, whose plant is in the background. *Gillig Corp.*

and pressed into service hundreds of retired buses. Outmoded buses that formerly served only on weekends of heavy travel and were driven not more than 10,000 miles a year now are being operated 75,000 to 100,000 miles annually. . . . These older buses, despite the most careful overhauling, do not provide the economy in the use of gas, oil and rubber that is obtained by the use of more modern equipment," according to *Intercity Buses at War*. During the war, the bus industry had trouble finding and retaining both drivers and especially mechanics.

However, programs dedicated to training bus drivers were in operation during World War II, such as one in Phoenix, Arizona:

New operator trainees were given 21 days of training. The program included three days of classroom work on laws, rules, complaints, and courtesy, as well as an orientation course in the mechanical structure of the buses they would be operating. Three days were spent on a practice course with an empty bus. Near the end of the practice course training, instructors often used a clever test to check for proper backing procedures. The instructor placed stack of nickels on a flat surface near the bus door. The new driver had to keep them from spilling while starting and stopping. After completing three practice days, the trainee spent at least four hours running on each route with a line inspector in order to get familiar with the system. (Source: Jerry W. Abbit, *History of Transit in the Valley of the Sun, 1887–1989*. Phoenix: The City of Phoenix Transit System, 1990.)

To better allocate resources to the war effort, nearly all sightseeing bus tours were eliminated. Carriers were also pressured into dropping or cutting back on bus service with a low load factor, or percent of capacity used.

Service men and women were more likely to be traveling on weekends with their passes, so bus company ads urged patrons to ride during weekdays. Some bus companies would call for service men and women to board first as they were loading their buses.

There was also a demand for buses to transport war workers during World War II. One articulated form of bus was the conventional tractor/semitrailer, converted from new car carriers with seats installed. It is worth noting that if the passengers had any questions for the driver, they were left unanswered because this arrangement separated the driver from the passengers.

Also during the war, small war-worker coaches were built by extending Chevrolet sedan chassis. The seating capacity of the unit was increased from 5 passengers to 12 with the addition of only 400 pounds of critical material. Chester Wardlow, in *The Transportation Corps: Responsibilities, Organization, and Operations*, notes that there were 910 buses of this type in service in August 1945.

When the war ended, there was great demand for new buses and even greater demand for new automobiles.

The 1947 *Silver Book* featured several ads. The Mid-State Body Company of Waterloo, New York, would convert 115-inch wheelbase Chevrolets to 146-inch wheelbase Campbell Commuter Station Wagons, which could carry 14 passengers. These vehicles looked like conventional Chevrolet station wagons except that they had one additional segment between the front and rear door. According to the ad, "The Campbell Commuter carries 11 to 14 passengers and the driver. Any and all of the seats are easily removed for emergency work. The Campbell Commuter can be sold for group transportation, emergency use, schools, and bus lines." On the opposing page was a continuation of Mid-State's ad, showing station wagon bodies on Chevrolet light truck chassis of 116-inch, 125-inch, 137-inch, and 161-inch lengths. In the same catalog is an ad from the National Body Manufacturing Co. of Knightstown, Indiana, listing "airport bus bodies," "panel body stretchouts for ambulances and funeral cars," and "pleasure car stretchouts for airport buses and funeral cars."

This 1941 Chevrolet bus was photographed in the 1980s in use at the Minnesota State Fair.

This same *Silver Book* featured ads for a number of school bus body builders, including Blue Bird Body Company of Fort Valley, Georgia; Carpenter Body Works of Mitchell, Indiana; H. O. De Boer and Associates of Lombard, Illinois; Hackney Bros. Body Co. of Wilson, North Carolina; Hicks Body Company of Lebanon, Indiana; Southern Aircraft Company of Garland, Texas; Superior of Lima, Ohio (which stated in the ad that the Lima body plant was a half-day's drive from Chevrolet's Norwood plant, where the chassis would be built); and Wayne of Richmond, Indiana.

The Pacific Car and Foundry Company's April 1949 *COACH*, a newsletter for customers, announced that its school bus bodies would now include a roof escape hatch. The article described why the feature was being offered. In 1947, an intercity transit bus had plunged into the Duwamish River near Renton, Washington. Water pressure blocked the doors, including the side escape door, making it impossible for passengers to escape. At the accident scene, rescuers cut a hole through the roof with an ax, and saved two passengers, although eight were killed. "Washington State patrolmen, who more than most other men know the perils of the highway, saw in that act a means of succor at similar disasters, and they suggested installation of roof hatches. The company agreed they were good and on its own initiative then followed through developing the roof escape hatch as it is today."

The war had generated additional business for intercity buses. Meier and Hoschek said 2,320 companies were operating 23,210 buses in 1945, carrying 950 million revenue passengers. The number of passengers had increased four times in five years. But by 1950, the number would drop to 655 million, due mainly to the automobile and, to a lesser extent, the airplane. Local transit ridership also dropped. As an extreme example, in Honolulu, between 1947 and 1948, ridership dropped from 84 million to 61 million. Streetcars and interurban trains disappeared from most cities.

A 1941 Dodge with a Thomas body. The sign by the door says "Have Fare Ready." Thomas bodies are made in High Point, North Carolina, where the firm started in 1916 as a builder of streetcars. Thomas Built Buses

There are two bus bodies here, one on the truck and one on the trailer. The truck-tractor is a GMC COE of the early 1940s. Note the two-color paint job with the stripe continuing between vehicles. This type of stripe was common just before World War II in an attempt to add "streamlined" patterns to squarish truck and bus bodies. This unit was built by Schult Trailers, Inc., of Elkhart, Indiana. American Truck Historical Society

Turlock, California, ran this 1941 White with a Gillig body. Note the overhead luggage rack and open spare tire compartment. Gillig Corp.

In Utica, New York, the last trolley service was operated on May 12, 1941, and Utica became an "all-bus" city. Just before World War II, the city purchased about 65 Twin Coaches, most of which were used to replace the rail system. After the war, they received 28 more. In 1948, the street railway reincorporated, and its new name was the Utica Transit Corporation. In Monterey, California, the Bay Rapid Transit received a potpourri of equipment: 10 Fords, 9 Flxibles, 5 Twin Coaches, 3 Whites, 2 Becks, and 1 Crown.

In 1942, Phoenix purchased 10 Crown coaches that were "air-cooled" for the riders' comfort. A high-speed Wisconsin engine pulled air through a duct system that ran through the bus. The system did not work well, and many argued at the time that air conditioning

in local buses would not work well because the doors were opened so frequently. The Phoenix bus system would not become fully equipped with air conditioned buses until the mid-1960s.

APTA estimates that by 1950, local transit buses were boarding about 9.4 billion passengers annually. Their peak year had been 1948, when they boarded 10.6 billion.

The Greyhound Silversides remained the intercity coach most associated with this era. General Motors made similar coaches for other bus lines. Other firms building intercity coaches also used the fluted metal siding on their products. General Motors dropped the Yellow Coach name for its buses in 1943; thereafter they were named "GMC."

A 15-passenger war-worker coach built on a 1942 Chevrolet passenger car chassis. Care was taken to use noncritical materials. The extended frame was of ash, and the extended roof was made of composition materials. *George C. Marshall Foundation*

Gillig built this Gray Lines Tour bus on a 1942 Ford chassis. *Gillig Corp.*

A World War II-vintage GMC tractor pulling a war-workers' semitrailer bus. The bus was built by Wentworth & Irwin, Inc., of Portland, Oregon. *Columbia Body & Equipment Co.*

This war-workers' bus, built on a semitrailer by Fruehauf, could carry 100 workers. The tractor is an International. *American Automobile Manufacturers Assn.*

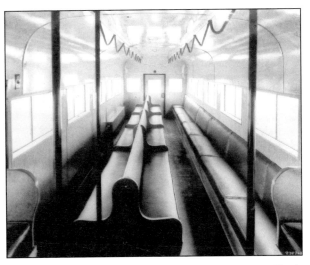

Inland Steel Co. used the Fruehauf trailer to carry workers during World War II. The roof slopes upward toward the front; it looks like there are steps up to seats above the fifth wheel. The trailer may have been converted from a new car carrier, which would help account for its shape. *Library of Congress*

The interior of a Schult war-workers' bus. *American Truck Historical Society*

Matson Navigation Company used this bus, built in the 1940s, to carry ship crews to and from the vessel. *Gillig Corp.*

The framework and roof are being finished on this Gillig bus. The chassis is a World War II-era GMC. Gillig Corp.

Spencer Trailer Company in Augusta, Kansas, made this trailer for use during World War II. The tractor is a Chevrolet. The Kansas State Historical Society, Topeka

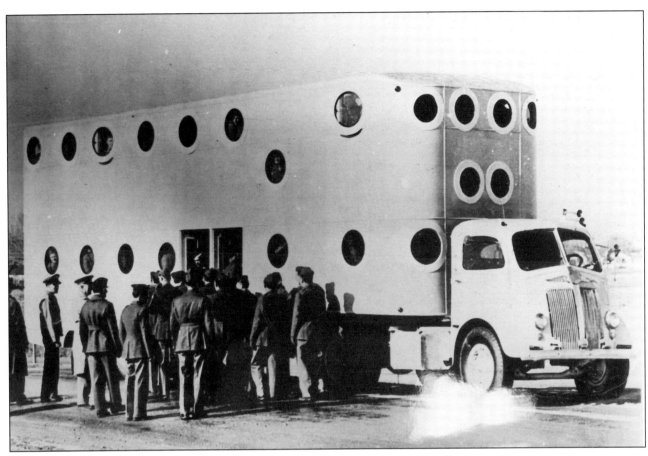

A wartime troop bus with two levels inside a semitrailer. The tractor is a White COE. Note the circular windows. There must be an interesting story, somewhere, explaining why they were circular.

This GM was built during World War II and likely went first to Greyhound. It is shown here in about 1950, in front of Heiser's Seattle truck and bus body shop, painted with Gray Line tour bus markings. Geo. Heiser Body Co.

This 1945 GMC Coach was originally purchased by the Missouri Pacific. It now belongs to the Pacific Bus Museum.

American Body & Equipment Co., in Dallas, built this school bus for Mineral Wells, Texas, on a 1940s Dodge chassis. It is painted several colors, probably red, white, and blue. *American Body & Equipment Co.*

In 1946, Kaiser built this articulated three-axle bus for carrying rail passengers between Los Angeles and Bakersfield, although later it served between Los Angeles and San Francisco. Special authority from the California Public Utilities Commission was required because passengers were being carried in a trailer. Santa Fe Trailways advertised this bus as "man-made magic." It was powered by a Cummins diesel mounted under the floor. The engine and transmission were mounted on a roller carriage that could be removed easily for service or replacement. *University of Akron Archives*

This 1947 A.C.F. Brill was spotted at a "Bus Bash" in Portland, Oregon. A.C.F. Brills were produced until the early 1950s.

A circa-1947 Dodge Power Wagon with a Gillig school bus body, used in northern California. *Gillig Corp.*

The interior of a 1947 Fageol Twin Coach, restored by the Monterey Salinas Transit agency, includes authentic advertising signs. *Monterey Salinas Transit*

This Greyhound "Silversides" was built in about 1947, and photographed in San Jose in 1997. The fluted pattern on the sides is made of aluminum, copied from streamlined railroad passenger coaches of the 1930s.

A postwar International Metro used as a crew bus by United Air Lines. American Automobile Manufacturers Assn.

A late 1940s REO with overhead luggage rack. Diamond REO Truck Sales, Winston-Salem, NC

Continental Trailways used this 1948 A.C.F. Brill, which was equipped with air conditioning. It was bound for Salt Lake City. *Institute of Transportation Studies, University of California*

Blue Bird buses have been built in Fort Valley, Georgia, since 1927. This was their first forward-control school coach, built in 1948. *Blue Bird Body Co.*

In 1947, Flxible had introduced an "Airporter" model to be used to carry passengers to and from airports. Seating was spacious, with a capacity of only 23 passengers. This is a 1948 Flxible "Airporter" at the Cleveland airport. The bus was powered by a Buick engine. *National Automotive History Collection, Detroit Public Library*

A 1948 Kenworth chassis was used for this bus, headed for Rainier National Park. *Paccar*

A Stewart bus body on a 1948-50 Ford. *Stewart Precision Corp.*

This is an exterior view of a small school bus on a late 1940s GMC chassis, built by Heiser of Seattle. *Geo. Heiser Body Co.*

Double-decked buses were never widely used in the United States. This 1950 A.E.C. was built in England. After it retired from its initial duties, it was shipped to the United States. It ended up in Davis, California, where it, and several other English double-deckers, are still in regular service, operated by the associated students at the University of California at Davis. In 1991, this bus was repowered with a Cummins diesel engine; it is now being converted to compressed gas power. *Unitrans, UC Davis*

This is a 1950 Carcoach, apparently built by Pacific Car & Foundry Co. for a short time to test the market for buses and vans of this size. A company newsletter suggested that potential uses could be school buses and for transporting logging crews. The initial production run was 10. *Paccar*

A small school bus built by Gillig on a circa-1950 Chevrolet chassis. *Gillig Corp.*

A 1950 International school bus with Arizona plates. *American Automobile Manufacturers Assn.*

CHAPTER SIX

1951-1960

During this decade, the nation's best-known bus driver was Ralph Cramden, played by Jackie Gleason on the TV hit series, *The Honeymooners*.

Also during this decade, Cummins Engine Company published a monthly magazine, *The Dependable Diesel*, which told about the introduction of diesel power into various applications. Some bus applications described included Continental Trailways, which tried Cummins diesel engines in two A.C.F.-Brill coaches in 1951. The company was sufficiently satisfied with the engines, and in 1952 ordered 33 new A.C.F.-Brills with Cummins power.

Another article started out:

One Sunday late in January 1956 was literally the end of the line for 49 streetcars in Dallas, Texas, as 49 new Southern Coach buses took to the street as their replacement. There were many nostalgic memories that went along with the passing of the streetcar. But Dallas gave a farewell party and then welcomed the buses with a mile long downtown parade. All of the new Southerns are powered by 200-horsepower Cummins diesels.

In the same issue was an article about a diesel-powered Crown school bus, used in Trona, near California's Death Valley. The school bus driver gave this testimonial:

I like the feeling of reserve power. No matter which direction we go from Trona, we have to make a pretty steep climb. The Cummins diesel makes all the grades easily, hauling 79 pupils. Another important thing is that we get nine miles per gallon from the fuel, whereas the best of the gasoline-powered buses will get only five miles per gallon. And so we use the diesel-powered bus on all the special trips. In that way I get to see a lot of ball games and attend most of the musical events. I drive for the high school teams, the band, glee club and other groups. Once I took a load of drama students to the Pasadena Playhouse, a round trip of about 300 miles. We didn't have to stop and go to the trouble of refueling.

A Gillig body on an early 1950s Chevrolet, used in Reno. *Gillig Corp.*

Air suspension systems, introduced in 1953, allowed the bus level to remain constant as its passenger load changed. Kenworth introduced a vehicle called the "Bruck," with a main deck divided into two sections, the front section for passengers, the rear, for freight. Potential customers were thought to be railroads who were trying to substitute highway for rail service in situations where regulatory bodies would not allow passenger service abandonments.

Buses were still subject to economic regulation by both state and federal agencies. In the following paragraph (which spans a few decades) are some excerpts from an article in the 1984 issue of *Snake River Echoes*

An open touring bus, used at Harpers Ferry. The canvas roof is elevated so people can stand up. The chassis is an early 1950s International. *State of West Virginia*

A 1951 Mack city bus used by San Francisco's municipal transit system. San Francisco was one of Mack's best bus customers in this era. Mack stopped building buses in 1960. *Institute of Transportation Studies, University of California*

about the Teton Stage Lines, in Idaho's Snake River Valley, and some of the steps in its expansion. Note that the expansion came about by acquiring other carriers' operating authorities.

In the mid-1940s, Albert Moulton of Driggs, Idaho, bought a small bus and obtained an Idaho Public Utilities Commission (PUC) permit to operate between Victor and Idaho Falls.

In the late 1940s, Moulton sold the line to Raymond Beckstead, who ran the line for five years, and began making some charter runs.

In 1953, the firm was purchased by Wells Grover, who had a school bus fleet but was restricted by the Idaho PUC in his use of school buses for other commercial purposes. By buying the Teton Stage Lines he received its permit from the Interstate Commerce Commission (ICC) to operate charters in three states.

In 1958, Greyhound wanted to give up its Idaho Falls-to-Ashton run to Grover because it was unprofitable. Local businesses didn't want to lose the nationally known Greyhound service and went to the regulatory agencies, and were able to block the Greyhound abandonment.

In the early 1960s, Grover wanted to expand his charter operations and did this by purchasing the Bear Lake Stage Lines, which had the ICC-given right to charter buses to anywhere in the U.S., and by the late 1960s the firm had 30 tour buses.

In the late 1950s, the Houghton Lake, Michigan, school district installed AM radios in its school buses with two speakers, one in the front and one in the rear. The local radio station scheduled a morning program called *School Bus Stop*, which would play records in response to mailed-in requests. Drivers said the radios "greatly reduced discipline problems and allowed them to monitor weather conditions," according to a historical article in *School Bus Fleet*.

The 1954 *Silver Book* carried ads for outfitters of school buses. Body builders with ads included the Blue Bird, Carpenter, Hackney Superior, and Wayne firms listed earlier. New listings were from Armbruster and Company, Fort Smith, Arkansas; National Body Mfg. Co., Knightstown, Indiana; Oneida Products Corp., Canastota, New York; Stewart Steel Products, Brooklyn, New York; Thomas Car Works, High Point, North Carolina; and Ward Body Works, Inc., Scone, Arkansas. That year, Chevrolet offered four school bus chassis wheelbases: 137, 161, 199, and 212 inches. A number of builders offered bodies to fit each, with an additional variant being the distance between rows of seats, which changed the seating capacity. The ad from Armbruster and Co. indicated that they were "builders of automobile extensions for over 25 years." Their ads showed Chevrolet sedans and station wagons extended to hold four rows of seats.

The U.S. Supreme Court's 1954 decision *Brown vs. Board of Education of Topeka* called for eliminating segregation in public schools. In many cities this meant massive use of busing students away from their neighborhood schools. The idea was to promote racial integration in schools and provide equal educational opportunities to children of all races.

In 1955, Rosa Parks refused to give up her seat on a Montgomery, Alabama, bus to a white man, resulting in a long boycott of the local bus system by Montgomery's blacks. The boycott showed that nonviolent demonstrations could be effective. The boycott also placed Martin Luther King Jr. into national prominence.

In 1959, Elvis Presley purchased a Flxible and had it customized for road tours by George Barris, the well-known southern California custom vehicle builder.

This GMC bus was used as a Greyhound "highway traveler" and subsequently was converted to a private coach.

Presley kept the bus until 1967 and often did the driving himself.

In 1958, U.S. airlines introduced jet aircraft into their scheduled service. Jets flew nearly twice as fast as propelled aircraft and as a result, the fly time between many cities decreased considerably. Jets also provided a smoother flight, which attracted passengers. This author, who was involved in airline matters before the Civil Aviation Board during this time, recalls witnesses testifying that air travel between specific cities would increase by 30 percent after jet service was introduced. These improvements in airline service increased the competitive advantage over buses and any rail passenger service that still remained.

The U.S. Transportation Act of 1958 made it easier for railroads to abandon passenger service, and the number of passenger trains dropped from 1,448 in 1958 to fewer than 500 a decade later. (These figures are from Robert Fellmeth, *The Interstate Commerce Omission*[sic]. These abandonments placed pressure on other forms of passenger transportation.

During this decade Utica Transit Corp., suffering from declining ridership and revenues, began retiring its gasoline-powered Twin Coaches, and replacing them with used diesel-powered GMs, purchased from other properties or leased from companies that specialized in used buses. In Monterey, California, the business of the Bay Rapid Transit Company was also declining, and during this decade it acquired five new GMs (including its first diesels) and two used Twin Coaches.

In *History of Mack Rail Motor Cars and Locomotives* with Randolph L. Kulp as editor, a report states that as of January 1, 1959, 26 aging Mack passenger rail motor cars were still in service on a total of 13 rail properties, including lines in Canada, Cuba, and Colombia.

Greyhound had emerged as the nation's primary intercity highway passenger carrier, and the firm and its affiliates operated over 5,000 buses (twice the number that they are operating today). Greyhound began to replace its Silversides with GM Scenicruisers. The Scenicruiser had a "vista dome" with higher seats in the rear. General Motors had dominant market shares of both the intercity and local transit markets. Well into the 1960s, the most prominent buses were the Scenicruiser and GM's various urban transit workhorses. By this time, most new intercity buses were equipped with small lavatories.

Crown built these two buses to carry both passengers and freight for Northern Pacific Transport. *Crown Coach Corp.*

Greyhound maintained a fleet of restored buses that it used for promotional purposes. From the far left is a 1954 Scenicruiser, a 1948 A.C.F. Brill, a 1947 Silversides, a 1937 GMC/Yellow Super Coach, a 1931 Mack, and a 1914 Hupmobile (Greyhound's first bus). Drivers are wearing uniforms of different vintages. *Greyhound Lines, Inc.*

By 1960, according to Meier and Hoschek, the intercity bus industry had reduced the number of firms to 1,150, less than half the number a decade earlier. Buses had dropped from 24,420 to 20,970 and revenue passengers to 366 million. Two developments during the decade, reported by Wren and Wren, were significant to the bus building industry. First, in 1957, in an antitrust action, the government forced Greyhound to break some of its long-standing ties with GM and find other sources for its buses. Secondly, various makes of buses started being imported from both Canada and Europe. In 1956, Continental Trailways began purchasing Setra Golden Eagle buses, built by Kässbohrer in Germany. The first order was for 200 units. Silver Eagles were produced shortly thereafter, and they were less luxurious. A number of bus builders dropped out of the market during the decade, leaving the field open to General Motors. According to the September 1961 issue of *Commercial Car Journal*, by the 1950s, GM "found itself, embarrassingly, almost in complete control of the bus market."

This was also the decade when the interstate highway system started. Eventually every major city in the nation would be linked with four-lane limited access highways. For freight markets, the interstate highway system nearly doubled the productivity of trucks; it prob-

ably had a similar effect on the bus/rail passenger markets. However, any advantages buses enjoyed would also be shared by autos traveling the same routes.

APTA estimated that by 1960, local transit buses, whose patronage had been declining steadily since 1948, were boarding about 6.4 billion passengers annually.

Southern Coach Manufacturing Co. of Evergreen, Alabama, built buses after World War II until about 1961. This is a demonstrator, built in 1954.

This 1950s Crown sightseeing bus was used in Hawaii. *Crown Coach Corp.*

A 1955-56 Dodge with a Superior school bus body. Dodge had difficulty competing in the heavy truck markets and was to drop out in the mid-1970s. *Superior Coach Division, Sheller Globe Corporation*

This bus-type body, built by Gerstenslager, was designed to carry a traveling chapel, and was used in North Carolina. Services could be held inside the bus, or a pulpit could placed at the opening for outdoor services. Gerstenslager is located in Wooster, Ohio. *Gerstenslager Corp.*

The Pacific Bus Museum owns this 1955 GMC, which was originally operated by Peerless Stages.

A 1956 Crown, used by Gray Line Tours of Chicago. It was air-conditioned. *Crown Coach Corp.*

Marmon-Herrington also built buses. This is a 1956 Marmon-Herrington city bus, used by the Denver Tramway Company. *Denver Regional Transportation District*

A Crown two-level sightseeing coach from the late 1950s. A 246-horsepower Hall Scott engine was in the middle under the floor. The bus seated 41 passengers on recliner seats. *Crown Coach Corp.*

Along the West Coast a variety of "hippie" vans appeared, often using old school bus bodies because of their generous interior dimensions. This chassis is a 1957 Ford. Toward the rear, one can see a chimney pipe sticking out a rear window. The top of the chimney is shown near the door—it's probably removed for highway travel. A carp kite hangs in front. This photo was taken in Sausalito, California.

A fleet of Crown school buses in the Pacific Northwest, circa 1957. Crown also was producing a line of fire apparatus at this time, and its buses and fire apparatus shared the same front-end sheet metal. *Crown Coach Corp.*

This 1958 GMC bus was sold to the Key System Transit Lines, which operated in the San Francisco Bay area. GM was the nation's primary—if not sole—supplier of buses during this era, and almost any urban street scene will show this model of bus. Over 38,000 were produced between 1940 and 1958. Today, these are known as the "old look" GMC buses. Some of the later ones had four headlights, rather than two. *John H. McKane*

A late 1950s Western Flyer, built in Winnipeg. This is one of the last intercity buses to have its engine mounted in front. The picture was taken at a "Bus Bash" in Portland, Oregon, after the bus had been converted to a private coach.

Tanner Gray Line Tours operated this late 1950s Crown in California. Its destination sign says: "Disneyland." *Crown Coach Corp.*

The interior shot of this 1950s Crown shows comfortable seats. *Crown Coach Corp.*

This 1959 GMC, used in the San Jose area, currently belongs to the Santa Clara Valley Transportation Authority.

A 1960 GMC Suburban now owned by Lester Hoffman Jr. of the Seattle area.

Transit officials inspect the first of a batch of circa-1960 GMC "new look" buses being delivered by rail to AC Transit, in Oakland, California. AC Transit

This long flatbed truck was outfitted to carry skiers in Rocky Mountain National Park from the parking area to the lifts. The skiers entered from the rear. Ski racks are mounted on the side. Rocky Mountain National Park

CHAPTER SEVEN

1961-1970

Commercial Car Journal, in its September 1961 issue, described the three facets of bus activity.

More than two-thirds of all buses (180,000) now [1961] haul kids to school . . . Biggest problems center in the paucity of operating funds and good management . . . Most of the managers are part-time teachers, individual owners, even senior students. Technically, few school buses are really buses at all. Rather, they are elongated truck chassis with school bus bodies. The future is bright indeed for the makers who can offer a rear-engine integral bus at a competitive price. Several are in the works now—and feature lower profile, more seats and greater safety.

Intercity buses have their share of problems too. Some are closely related to the ills of rail passenger service, i.e., the necessity to maintain fixed schedules over

Pictured is an overturned school bus in the 1960s. Note that the left side emergency door is open, used to allow passengers to escape. *Crown Coach Corp.*

fixed routes, many of which have low income potential. Biggest enemy of both is the private passenger car.

Buses in city transit face a tough, but far from hopeless, future. Born of necessity, they will survive of necessity, if the city itself is to survive. The biggest headache centers on modern "downtown" which is at the same time more congested and less centralized than before. More people go downtown in private autos (creating the congestion) but fewer people go downtown at all. To add to the confusion, some cities—like Los Angeles—have grown in so many directions there's hardly a downtown left. Any way you slice it, transit loses.

In the early 1960s for service between Los Angeles and San Francisco, Continental Trailways used five articulated Eagle buses, all of which were removed from

A 1961 Flxible city bus. *Flxible*

service because of maintenance problems. One was sold to the Alameda-Contra Costa Transit District and used for commute runs across the Bay Bridge.

A Bureau of Public Roads study of highway speeds on rural highways showed that buses operated at higher speeds than either autos or trucks. In the Eastern United States, the buses operated at an average speed of 54.4 miles per hour; in the Central and West, 59.6 miles per hour, for a nationwide average of 57.7 miles per hour. The nationwide average speed for automobiles was 56.9 miles per hour and for trucks, 51.1 miles per hour. These figures are from *Motor Trucks in the Metropolis*.

Meier and Hoschek said that the number of intercity bus companies had dropped to 1,000 by 1970, operating 22,000 buses, while the number of revenue passengers was up from a decade earlier to 401 million.

Railroad passenger traffic had been on a downward spiral since the end of World War II. The Transportation Act of 1958 made it easier for railroads to abandon passenger service, which they claimed was hurting them financially. By about 1970, it became necessary for the federal government to step in and form Railpax, whose name was soon changed to Amtrak. Amtrak became a government passenger railroad which still runs to this day. In the northeast Amtrak approximately breaks even in the routes between Washington, DC, New York City, and Boston. In the rest of the country, it offers sparse scheduled service and is highly subsidized. At times, Amtrak's opponents calculated that it would be cheaper to give every Amtrak passenger a free bus ticket and close down the rail operation.

Local bus systems were faced with many problems.

After the end of World War II, private ownership of automobiles skyrocketed. With the possible exception of New York City, owning an automobile was commonplace, and riders aboard public transit were becoming second-class citizens.

Surveys taken aboard public vehicles in various cities over the years show that the vast majority, in a range of 71 to 95 percent, of the people interviewed were there because they couldn't drive, because they did not own a car, or because the car they did own was in the garage. The surveys show that public transportation in American is the carrier of last resort. That means, all too often, that public transportation is hell on wheels. (Source: John Burby, *The Great American Motion Sickness, or Why You Can't Get There From Here*. Boston: Little, Brown, 1971.)

In major federal legislation in 1964, the federal government made massive capital grants to help cities with their transit systems. The most frequent use of the grant was for the city to buy out a private bus property and substitute a public transit agency in its place.

The city of Phoenix and American Transit [the private operator] formed a new organizational system, whereby the city took ownership and control of the bus system and PTS [Phoenix Transit System, a private entity apparently owned by American Transit] contracted to manage the system based on an established fee. Immediately, processes began for submission of a grant application to the Urban Mass Transit Administration (UMTA) for the purchase of 55 new buses. (Source: Jerry W. Abbit,

Head-on view of a school bus on a 1961 International chassis.

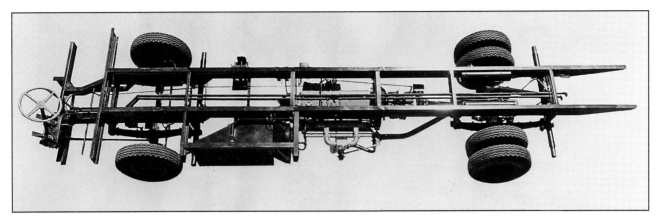

This is a Crown chassis for a controls-forward bus. The power plant is below the frame, with the cooling intake on the driver's side. Crown Coach Corp.

History of Transit in the Valley of the Sun, 1887–1989. Phoenix: The City of Phoenix Transit System, 1990.)

The properties purchased typically consisted of worn-out buses and unionized drivers and mechanics whose contracts also had to be honored by the new public operator. The massive infusion of federal money ultimately resulted in nearly a complete replacement of the nation's urban bus fleet. Federal funds came with some strings attached, including a requirement that the vehicle, or substantial parts, be made in the United States. That rule explains part of the reason for foreign-based bus builders locating operations in the United States.

In Utica, the city's government organized the Utica Transit Commission, a public agency, to take over and run the city's buses. There was some debate over whether the suburbs, which had been receiving bus service, were obligated to help with the government subsidies to the city. The commission bought five new GMC buses in 1967 and in 1969 received a federal grant to buy 27 more. In Monterey, California, the Bay Rapid Transit Company held on, acquiring 14 GMCs, apparently all used.

In 1968, the Urban Mass Transportation Administration (UMTA) was transferred from the Department of Housing and Urban Development to the Department of Transportation. In the last half of the decade, there was considerable interest in the problem of emissions from various motor vehicles. Steps were taken to reduce the emissions and to experiment with "alternative" fuels. UMTA soon also encouraged development of a "Transbus," which would be lower and designed to attract riders away from their autos. Ultimately, only two builders, GM and Flxible, developed buses that met the Transbus specifications, and soon the Flxibles developed structural problems. APTA estimated that by 1970, local transit buses were boarding about 5.0 billion passengers annually. It appeared the massive infusions of public funds were having little effect in attracting riders.

The 1968 *Silver Book* contained ads for the following school bus body builders: Automotive Conversion Co. of Troy, Michigan; Blue Bird; Boyertown Auto Body Works of Boyertown, Pennsylvania; Carpenter; Coach & Equipment Sales of Penn Yan, New York; Franklin Body & Equipment Corp. of Brooklyn, New York; National Coaches, Inc., of Knightstown, Indiana; Superior; Thomas; Union City Body Co. of Union City, Indiana; Ward; and Wayne. Most of these firms were also listed as suppliers of passenger buses as was Flxible Southern Company of Evergreen, Alabama, a subsidiary of the Flxible Co. of Loudonville, Ohio.

For many years, bus bodies have been outfitted with living accommodations for use as the ultimate camper. Both new and old buses can be so equipped, and the term used to describe them is "private coach." Some traveling entertainers use these buses, and some house movie stars when a film is being shot in an isolated area. A small number of tour coaches are equipped with bunks so the passengers can sleep while in transit.

The 1960s was a very unsettled decade in terms of politics and society. Hippies challenged conventional social behavior. In Washington, Oregon, and northern California, one could spot "hippiemobiles" in which hippies traveled and lived. These were made from recycled delivery vans or school buses. They were painted colorfully, to say the least, and often sported a stovepipe. "Deadheads"—Grateful Dead fans—frequently lived in old school buses that had been converted to traveling homes.

In *Rolling Homes, Handmade Houses on Wheels*, a book on these conversions, is a description of how an owner converted his late 1950s International school bus:

> Buses have a distinctive form that is not found on a flatbed truck. The shell is convenient as a temporary shelter, but converting a bus into a comfortable, spacious and well-lit house usually means raising the roof. With no

Carpenter school buses have been built in Mitchell, Indiana, since 1919, although the firm's first products were horse-drawn. This is a Carpenter assembly line, photographed in 1963. At that time, the firm's sales motto was: "The safest link between home and school." *Carpenter Body Works, Inc.*

previous building experience, Jonathan began remodeling his school bus with some help from his friends. A welder raised the roof, and Jonathan claims the rest was common sense. Skylights admit plenty of light and leave enough wall space for artistic displays. The banks of bus windows are well-positioned for cross ventilation and allow the sun to heat the bus.

The "Green Tortoise" bus line went into operation. It would take its passengers on leisurely trips, sometimes relying on majority votes of the passengers to determine the routes and times. The Green

Tortoise exists today, with its 1998 Web site listing saying, in part:

There is no shower on the bus, but we do stop at campgrounds or other public facilities. It's not possible to have a shower every day, but we swim many days and take no-soap showers in waterfalls, etc. There in no toilet—or chemical smell—on the bus and we stop frequently for restroom breaks and for the comfort of our smokers. Sometimes when we're far from civilization, we employ the Tortoise—and forest agency—approved method of 'shovel behind bush.'

A Crown bus with twin rear axles, used in Grand Teton National Park. *Crown Coach Corp.*

A 1963 Ford bus utilized by the U.S. Army to carry trainees. *U.S. Army Transportation Museum, Fort Eustis*

Exterior and interior shots of a circa-1960s Crown "security" bus used by the sheriff in San Joaquin County, California, to transport prisoners. (A 1994 article in *Corrections Today* said that the Los Angeles County Sheriff's office has a fleet of 75 buses and 30 vans and sedans used for prisoner transport.) *Crown Coach Corp.*

A 1964 Ford with a Superior school bus body. Superior Coach Division, Sheller Globe Corporation

A mid-1960s GMC "new look" transit bus that has been converted to a private coach. In this period, GM continued to dominate the market for both city and intercity buses. Over 22,000 "new look" buses were built between 1959 and 1977.

The Army utilized a bus body for an ambulance that could be outfitted with seats or stretchers. U.S. Army Transportation Museum, Fort Eustis

A Crown intercity coach built to carry the U.S. Air Force Band. Crown Coach Corp.

School buses were some of the first buses to be equipped with wheelchair lifts. This Crown bus was built for Pasadena in 1965. The elevator door is at the right rear. Crown Coach Corp.

This view shows the Passadena Crown bus doors open and elevator at ground level. The operator is holding the controls. The rear of the bus was the area set aside for wheelchairs and their riders. Tie downs for the wheelchairs were necessary when the bus was in motion. *Crown Coach Corp.*

This Ford C-series was used at the Zurich airport to carry passengers between the terminal and their airplane. Double doors allowed for quick movement of passengers. It's now on display at the Swiss National Transport Museum in Lucerne.

This is a Superior body on a mid-1960s GMC school bus chassis. *Superior Coach Division, Sheller Globe Corporation*

A retired International school bus from the 1960s has been converted into a traveling food vending rig. Midway toward the rear is a counter, closed solid windows, and a rolled-up shade.

A Crown bus made for use in Yellowstone National Park. Crown Coach Corp.

This view looks inside the rear luggage compartment of the Crown bus pictured above. Crown Coach Corp.

A Crown school bus with twin rear axles built for Palos Verdes, California, in 1966. One of the two mirrors on the corner allows the driver to see the front bumper and area in front of it. Crown Coach Corp.

A circa-1968 GMC converted to a private coach. A small Honda automobile fits in the open compartment and uses the ramps.

San Francisco's MUNI still owns this 1969 Flxible.

A circa-1970 GMC used by a church in Boron, California. Used school buses are often bought by churches for use in their youth programs.

CHAPTER EIGHT

1971-1980

By the mid-1970s, articulated buses were introduced in a number of urban transit markets. Their principal advantage was and continues to be one of reducing the labor costs per passenger. In 1976, GM introduced its "kneeling" bus, which could lower its entrance door by evacuating air from the right front suspension.

Some of the new public transit agencies supplemented their earnings by chartering their unused buses, which competed with private operators. However, private operators worked to get federal rules changed so that some public transit agencies could not charter buses for use outside their usual service areas.

There were several fuel "crises" during this decade. Along with gas shortages, there were waiting lines at service stations, and the retail prices of gasoline doubled. A nationwide speed limit of 55 miles per hour resulted in intercity coach schedule changes.

APTA estimated that in 1971, local transit buses were boarding about 4.7 billion passengers annually. Because of the fuel crisis, this number would climb to 5.2 million in 1976. (At that time, APTA changed its definition of "passenger trip" and later data is not comparable.)

An early 1970s GMC "new look" bus propelled by steam and used by AC Transit. This steam engine was developed by William M. Brobeck of Berkeley. It was one of three buses tested in a study for reducing exhaust emissions by buses. The drawback turned out to be fuel consumption which was two to three times higher than that of a comparable diesel-powered bus. *AC Transit*

Because of the increased gasoline prices, it appeared that bus and van travel would become more popular. At the end of the decade Lester R. Brown, Christopher Flavin, and Colin Norman, in *The Future of the Automobile in an Oil-Short World*, concluded: "In the United States, automobile sales are down and travel habits are changing. Ridership on public transportation has turned sharply upward in 1979. Motorists are leaving their cars in record numbers, as public transportation is upgraded and as gasoline prices climb."

Urban bus operators earned extra revenue by renting out ad space both inside and outside their buses. The interior ads would be seen by riders, the exterior ads would be viewed by motorists or pedestrians. A firm selling ad space on southern California buses during the late 1970s, when both buses and bus ridership were increasing, said this in one of their booklets:

The youth market, perhaps the most sought after demographic, is easily and effectively reached by transit advertising. There is figuratively, if not literally, a bus stop and transit route outside every high school, college and

A fancy Superior body on an International chassis, circa 1971. There are no school bus markings. This bus must be intended for a commercial market. *Superior Coach Division, Sheller Globe Corporation*

university in Southern California. The beaches and other sources of young adult concentrations are also well served by transit.

This was the decade when "demand-responsive" public transportation was first introduced. The potential rider would call in by telephone and a ride would be scheduled. A small van equipped with a radio would arrive at the rider's door and pick him or her up. The van might contain other riders as well. Riders would be taken to their respective destinations. If it was late at night, the van driver would keep his spotlight on the patron until the patron was safely inside his or her dwelling. Today the service is often called "dial-a-ride" or "demand-responsive." It is used primarily for transporting disabled individuals, or to transport individuals in areas where passengers are too sparse to fill a regular bus. The APTA estimates that there are over 5,200 transit agencies in the United States that currently (1996) offer demand-responsive service. Federal regulations have also begun requiring wheelchair accessibility on regular-size transit buses that were purchased with federal funds.

Van pools became more common. They were set up to carry groups of commuters to and from work. Often the employer subsidized the pool by providing free parking at the job site, or helping with insurance or vehicle payments. Many times tax laws encouraged employers to assist with van pools. Usually one driver owned and operated the vehicle—typically a van—and the other riders paid him or her on a contractual basis. Riders had some leverage in demanding certain qualities of service. Van pool vehicles generally had more comfortable seating and amenities than would be found on a bus.

One example today are the four or five full-size "club" buses that go to and from the United Airlines Maintenance base, near San Francisco's airport, and one of the largest employers in the Bay area. The driver/owner of each bus is also employed by United, and works a full shift at the base. The Golden Gate Bridge District subsidized some "club buses" used for commute purposes.

The 1974 *Silver Book* contained ads for the following school bus body builders: Automotive Conversion Co.; Blue Bird; Boyertown Auto Body Works; Carpenter; Coach & Equipment Sales; Franklin Body & Equipment Corp.; National Custom Coaches, Inc., of Knightstown, Indiana; Superior; Thomas; Union City Body Co.; and Wayne. This edition of the *Silver Book* indexed many other categories of bus bodies including activity buses, airport buses, charter buses, church and Sunday School buses, day camp buses, factory buses, invalid buses, jitney buses and buses for the handicapped, motel buses, private day care buses, sightseeing buses, ski resort buses, suburban buses, and work crew buses. A few additional bus body builders listed under these categories included Chef's Campers, Inc., of Seattle, Washington; Flxible Southern; Olson Corp. of Garden City, New York; Parsons Customs Products of Parsons, Kansas; and Time Savers, Inc., of Sacramento, California.

Federal assistance to urban mass transit operations increased and remained at relatively stable levels during this decade. The federal government assisted by paying up to 80 percent of capital costs and 50 percent of operating costs. By this time, it was generally believed that bus builders, bus drivers, and mechanics working for public agencies were the primary beneficiaries of these federal funds. Buses were far less costly than adding new

A mid-1970s Ford that has been converted to a mobile X-ray unit and is used in Miami. Note the roof has been raised.

rail systems. Yet many transit planners advocated rail systems because of the belief they would ultimately attract more riders. In addition, politicians preferred rail systems because they generated more publicity and local construction jobs.

Utica's Transit Commission Authority was re-created as the Utica Transit Authority and it was supposed to have a regional, rather than city, outlook. During this decade, Utica purchased no transit buses.

In Monterey, a public transit agency called Monterey Peninsula Transit was formed, and took the place of Bay Rapid Transit Co. Frank Lichtanski, in the January 1980 issue of *Motor Coach Age*, described the public agency's first days.

> To preclude any interruption of service, six poorly maintained [GMC] TDH-4517s were leased (later to be purchased) from El Paso City Lines; at the time Bay Rapid Transit needed four buses to maintain peak-hour schedules and three buses in midday hours. The buses arrived in town on September 19, 1973.
>
> Bay Rapid Transit Co. operated its last transit service on September 25, 1973. On the next day the Monterey Peninsula Transit replaced the company's system with an identical one, and on that day four of its six buses broke down. Operating from a corner of the city of Pacific Grove's maintenance yard, Monterey Peninsula Transit had no repair facilities, tools, parts, or mechanics, having purchased only some benches and fareboxes from Bay Rapid Transit. A deal with a local service station for bus maintenance soon failed. A bus had to be leased from Bay Rapid Transit, which was still in the charter and sightseeing business, and two school buses were borrowed from the county.

During the balance of the decade, Monterey Peninsula Transit acquired 20 used GMCs from other properties, mainly via leases. It also acquired 2 minibuses and 15 new Flxibles, replacing the leased GMCs.

In 1974, Minnesota became the last state to adopt the use of "school bus yellow" (technically known as "National School Bus Chrome"). Until that time, Minnesota's color had been "Minnesota Golden Orange."

School bus safety had been a perplexing problem since the 1960s with political figures such as Ralph Nader becoming critics of the industry. Massive new federal regulations regarding safety equipment came into effect in the mid-1970s. All school buses produced since 1977 meet these standards. Subsequently, ads for used school buses indicated whether the bus met the 1977 standards. All advertising literature regarding school bus bodies stressed safety features. Wayne literature offers an example of its emphasis on school bus safety features:

- Full-length metal panels extending the length of the body; stronger than short panels, they offered fewer seams to be broken and fewer sharp edges to be exposed in case of an accident from the side.
- Full-length interior panels, to eliminate "cookie cutter" seams; all surface edges were "turned, rounded, or closed off to shield the passengers."
- "Space-age" fasteners, rather than bolts or rivets, "the same type of bolt used for joining major structurals of spacecraft, skyscrapers, and girder joints of major buildings that must resist seismic forces."
- The frame design and the five different gauges of metal used for reinforcement provided greater protection during roll-overs and in rear-impact collisions.
- Larger windows provided a means of escape if the bus went on its side.
- A buzzer would sound if the rear escape door was unlatched while the bus ignition was on.
- The driver had a large windshield and a special console for controlling lights.
- Passenger seats were anchored to standards exceeding the federal requirements, and seat backs were padded to protect students in an accident.
- Antirust protection helped preserve the body and its features.

A not-so-subtle statement in the booklet said that school districts were buying the Wayne body "to maximize safety and put themselves in the strongest position for *accountability* in event of an accident."

As a whole, the bus industry had a good reputation for safety. In the early 1970s, the National Association of

Motor Bus Owners looked at fatality statistics for the years 1970–1972. The fatality rate for Class I (gross revenues over $1 million) bus lines was .09 deaths for every 100 million passenger miles. This was slightly better than the airlines, with a rate of .10. Rates for passenger rails were .28 and automobiles, 2.0. New regulations for intercity coaches allowed them to restrict smokers to seats in the rear.

According to National Association of Motor Bus Owners estimates, the nation's bus fleet in 1973 included 320,000 school buses, 48,300 local transit buses, 22,300 intercity and suburban buses, and 18,000 sightseeing and airport buses. In 1973, a total of 1,000 different firms were performing intercity bus transportation, although only 71 had gross revenues of over $1 million. The association also reported that in 1973, the intercity and suburban buses performed 385 million person trips (carrying one passenger on one trip), while the domestic airlines performed 185 million, and Amtrak, 17 million.

Little has been said about trams in this book. A piece of literature issued in the late 1970s by Microbus Corporation of Downey, California, listed and illustrated several trams and tram trains. Some units consisted of a power unit with seats, pulling matched sets of two or three trailers, capable of carrying over 150 persons. Many had outward-facing seats from which passengers would descend. A special tractor was designed to look like a steam locomotive; and some separate powered cars were designed to look like San Francisco cable cars. The firm also built conventional medium and small bus bodies.

This was the decade when the phrase "mobility rights" came into use, and it had at least two applications. For the physically disabled, it meant a right to being able to travel on mainstream transportation wherever and whenever they wanted. Over the past few decades, at considerable expense, the nation's bus system has gradually become accessible to disabled riders in most markets.

The other less common use of "mobility rights" was applied to residents of rural areas who were without automobiles, but who felt that government had an obligation to provide them with public transportation. With federal assistance, many counties set up public transit systems serving rural areas and hamlets. This was a softer approach to a problem than one taken with another rural issue in the past, when some counties actually zoned rural land areas to outlaw year-round residents, to avoid the costs of providing school bus services to residents in remote rural locations.

A 1975 AM General operated by San Francisco's MUNI mass transit system. AM General's headquarters were located in Wayne, Michigan.

A 1975 Flxible used by AC Transit. It's followed by a GMC "new look" bus. *AC Transit*

The constructing of the rear of a Superior school bus body during the 1970s. *Superior Coach Division, Sheller Globe Corporation*

A Superior school bus body on an International chassis, from the late 1970s. *Superior Coach Division, Sheller Globe Corporation*

This Carpenter school bus body is being placed on a chassis in 1978. The firm's sales brochure pointed out that the body was sufficiently strong to support its own weight. *Carpenter Body Works, Inc.*

A late 1970s German-built Mercedes bus used by Allegheny Commuter Airlines. *Allegheny Airlines*

A 1979–80 GMC Rapid Transit Series demonstrator. *Nova Bus Corp*

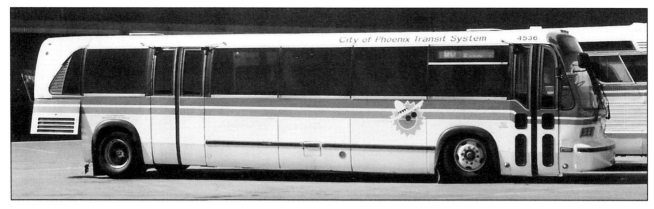

This 1979 GMC was used by the Phoenix Transit System. *Phoenix Public Transit Department*

A 1979–83 Motor Coach Industries (MCI) intercity bus photographed in 1985. MCI buses were originally built in Winnipeg, although some assembly operations have been moved to the United States, with its main offices being in Des Plaines, Illinois.

A circa-1980 GMC diesel built by General Motors Diesel Division Ltd. of Canada and used in Montreal. *Nova Bus Corp.*

CHAPTER NINE

1981-1990

In *Modern Intercity Coaches*, Larry Plachno wrote: "The decade of the 1980s will probably be remembered by the American intercity bus industry for at least four things: wider buses, longer and articulated buses, deregulation, and the arrival of imported buses from Europe."

European-built buses became more popular because they were more luxurious than U.S.-built equipment, and apparently were preferred by the tour bus customers. During this decade, the United States attracted tourists from both Europe and Asia as the value of the dollar sank in relation to other currencies. In the urban transit market—subsidized by the federal government—a number of suppliers were also foreign-based, although final assembly was performed in the United States in order to meet "local content" requirements. Even some school buses had foreign roots. Literature circa 1990 featured the TAM-USA school bus, built in Slovenia "along the Southern slope of the Austrian Alps" and with an exclusive distributor located in Van Nuys, California.

Wheelchair loading ramp on an early 1980s AM General. *AM General*

Whichever bus is considered the "representative" bus of this era, we know for certain that it was not totally "made in the U.S.A."

Early in the decade, the Utica Transit Authority purchased 29 Orion buses, made in upstate New York by the offshoot of a Canadian firm.

During this decade, some U.S. truck manufacturers developed alliances with European truck builders who also produced buses. One example was White and Volvo; another was Mack and Renault. In 1985, Mack introduced its FR-1 motorcoach, which combined a Renault coach body with a Mack power train, to U.S. markets.

The U.S. Bus Regulatory Reform Act of 1982 followed the trend of removing bus carriers from regulatory shackles, opening markets to competition, and making it easier for buses to withdraw from money-losing markets . As a result, service abandonments in small towns increased. Some of Greyhound's difficulties can be attributed to this law, since competitors could now enter into Greyhound's lucrative markets, on which the company had depended to subsidize service to less profitable markets.

The entire decade proved to be difficult for Greyhound, now faced with new competition from nonunion carriers. The company made several attempts to cut employees' wages, and a strike in 1983 included some violence. In 1986, Greyhound again attempted to cut wages, citing competition from the newly deregulated airline industry. Greyhound management announced that if the employees did not agree to the salary cuts, it would sell the division. The union rejected these demands, and Greyhound sold its bus division. The new owner announced that it had bought only the buses and the Greyhound name, but not the work force. Later in the decade, Greyhound took over Trailways, which had been fighting bankruptcy.

Buses changed their appearance as well. New intercity coaches no longer had the metallic fluting along their sides, introduced on the Greyhound Silversides before World War II, but now had flat metal sides.

Two major school bus accidents in the late 1980s in Carrollton, Kentucky, and Alton, Texas, claimed over 20 fatalities each. After investigations, federal school bus safety regulations were tightened, with new regulations covering use of flammable materials inside the bus, and the placement of emergency exits.

Manufacturers offered a wide variety of school bus chassis sizes. Chevrolet's 1981 full-size school bus chassis had wheelbase lengths of 149, 189, 218, 235, 254, and 274 inches; its intermediate size chassis had wheelbases of 125, 133, and 157 inches; and it also offered a "cutaway van" bus chassis on a 125-inch wheelbase. The "cutaway" had the van's front end and cab with a larger bus body fitted behind. Chevrolet also offered conventional vans, which could seat 16 students or 12 adults, and their Suburban model, with the warning that the Suburban did "not meet National School Bus Standards."

By 1984, the contents of the *Silver Book* had changed and a large proportion of its listings were for camper and van bodies. It contained ads for the following school bus body builders: Blue Bird; Carpenter; Thomas; and Wayne. This edition of the *Silver Book* indexed two other categories of bus bodies: activity buses and buses for the handicapped.

Bus builders listed under these categories included Armbruster/Stageway; Braun Corporation of Winamac, Indiana, Champion Home Builders, Dryden, Michigan; ElDorado Motor Corp., Minneapolis, Kansas; FLX, Inc., Evergreen, Alabama; Gresham Driving Aids of Wixom, Michigan;

A circa-1981 Blue Bird forward-control school coach. *Blue Bird Body Co.*

National Seating Company of Michigan, Fraser, Michigan; Tech-Trans, Bristol, Indiana; Tra-Tech Corp., Fort Worth, Texas; Turtle Top of Goshen, Indiana; and Van Epoch, Inc., of Romeo, Michigan. (While the *SilverBook* dealt only with Chevrolet bodies, most small- and medium-size bus bodies could fit on GMC, Ford, Dodge, and International chassis as well.)

The decade was marked by considerable federal expenditures for public mass transit, and continual disagreement between supporters of bus and rail systems. Buses were more fuel- and cost-efficient, but potential users found them less attractive than rail systems.

The Reagan administration attempted to reduce government's role in everyday economic life through "privatization"—returning operations to the private sector. As an example, the San Francisco Bay area's rail transit system, BART, had contracts with some public bus operations to feed passengers to and from BART rail stations. These contracts were given to private-sector bus operators. Public bus companies also began to farm out some maintenance operations to private firms.

The allowable vehicle width for operating on highways was increased from 96 to 102 inches. This benefited truckers primarily, although most coach builders also incorporated this new width into their new models, which increased the spaciousness inside coaches.

APTA estimates that by 1990, local transit buses were boarding about 5.7 billion passengers annually, down slightly from 1980. However, this figure is not strictly comparable to data from earlier periods.

Carpenter Cavalier

A 1981 Carpenter Cavalier forward-control school bus with a front-mounted engine. The Corsair model was also forward controlled, but had a rear-mounted engine. In very recent years, Carpenter has begun using the Crown name for its school buses. *Carpenter Body Works, Inc.*

Right Page
Greyhound has became a major customer of Motor Coach Industries. Here is an early 1980s MC-9. According to an investor-oriented news item on the World Wide Web, in mid-1998, Greyhound entered into a 10-year agreement with MCI to give MCI at least 80 percent of its new bus orders. *Greyhound Lines, Inc.*

The Tri-County Metropolitan Transportation District, centered in Portland, Oregon, ran this 1981 Ikarus transit bus. It was one of an order of 87. Ikarus buses are built in Budapest, Hungary, and, in the early 1980s, Crown imported them and finished them to U.S. standards. (They did enough work on them in the United States to meet the "local content" requirements for buses bought with federal assistance.) Since then, the Ikarus firm has been included in a newer firm, known as North American Bus Industries. *Tri-Met, Portland*

A 1982 Wayne "Busette" school bus body on a Chevrolet chassis. Literature indicated that the body could fit on a Chevrolet, Ford, or GMC chassis. *Wayne Corporation*

The Phoenix Transit System ran this 1983 Flxible. *Phoenix Public Transit Department*

Boise Urban Stages uses this 1983 Gillig.

A Ward school bus body on an early 1980s GMC chassis, spotted in Hannibal, Missouri. Mirrors in front allow the driver to see alongside and directly in front of the bus. The first Ward bus was built in 1933, and they are still being built in Conway, Arkansas, by the American Transportation Corporation.

Kent State University operates this mid-1980s MCI. *Kent State University*

An intermediate-size bus built by ElDorado Motor Corporation of Minneapolis, Kansas, which began building buses in 1977. *ElDorado Motor Corp.*

Vinyl wrap was used on this 1987 Flxible to advertise a Florida restaurant. *Broward County Mass Transit Division*

An ElDorado body on a Ford chassis, circa 1987. Options included a TV and VCR, restroom, and kitchenette. Seating was either around the inside perimeter of the body, or in conventional rows with an aisle in the middle. *ElDorado Motor Corp.*

CHAPTER TEN

1991 TO THE PRESENT

The exterior appearance of some buses changed dramatically during this decade. Vinyl wrap, which could completely enclose a bus without impairing the passengers' view, was used to advertise soft drinks and tourist attractions. (Advertising signs both inside and outside of buses had always been a source of revenue for bus operators.)

Star Trax Industries, which supplies buses for use by entertainers, said in a recent ad: "Conceive the magnitude of 'coach wraps.' The 'wraps' are graphics which fully encompass the coach; all 45 feet in length and 13 feet 3 inches in height. Needless to say, they are the topic of conversation wherever these coaches roll. 'Incredible' results, Warner Lambert said after the completing its Dentyne Ice summer campaign."

Air travel continued to grow, and while this had an impact on intercity bus operations, it also generated a huge demand for bus operations to and from airports. Step outside a terminal today, and you will see a parade of buses going downtown, to suburbs, to car rental lots, to parking lots, and to nearby hotels.

The Americans with Disabilities Act of 1993 enabled more disabled people to be a part of mainstream society. Bus operators were now highly encouraged to provide buses with wheelchair lifts and other equipment in terminals and at stops necessary to accommodate the disabled. Some transit systems increased their offerings of dial-a-ride or demand-responsive services with small specialized buses. Some disabled people disliked the smaller vehicles and specialized equipment, feeling that it segregated them from mainstream travelers. In early 1998, the U.S. Secretary of Transportation proposed a rule that would require all commercial bus lines to be fully accessible to wheelchair riders by the year 2112.

There is another group of riders, not considered disabled, but requiring nearly the same services. They are the elderly, who can still perform all their functions, but

This 1991 New Flyer low-floor bus is used at Kennedy International Airport. The destination sign says: "Long Term," referring, no doubt, to a parking lot. The New Flyer firm was founded in 1986, when a Dutch firm acquired the Flyer Industries Ltd. from the government of Manitoba. One advantage of low-floor buses is that, if it is a bus that contains the "kneeling" feature (i.e., air is let out of right front suspension), no ramp is needed at most curbsides. *Port Authority of New York and New Jersey*

are slower and more fragile than they once were. Demand-responsive bus systems are provided for their needs as well, with van-like vehicles that often have wheelchair lift and raised roofs.

One of the major complaints of school bus operators in the 1990s was behavior of their passengers.

An articulated, early 1990s North American Bus Industries bus used by the Miami-Dade Transit Agency. *Bobbie C. Crichton*

An article in the February 1995 issue of *School Bus Fleet* said:

> Of all the changes contractors, districts and drivers mention when they talk about the challenges of their profession, this is the one they feel has changed, and for the worst, over the past 30 years. Today's youths don't stay in their seats; they fight and throw things at each other and out the windows; they swear like Marines; and they won't do what the driver asks them to do. Gangs, weapons, students sexually harassing other students, drugs, fights: those are all problems on buses today.

In the magazine were ads for products to protect bus surfaces from graffiti, kits for testing drivers' breath and saliva for alcohol, and video cameras for continually recording passenger activity and behavior aboard the bus.

Those riding in an automobile are now required by law to wear a seat belt. Although wearing seat belts would be difficult to enforce on many types of buses, school buses are another story. At present there is considerable disagreement regarding the use of seat belts on school buses. At the moment, only two states, New Jersey and New York, require wearing seat belts on new school buses.

During this decade, interest in alternative fuels developed, mainly to curb air pollution. The Clean Air Act of 1990 required private fleets of 10 or more vehicles that were centrally fueled to phase in clean-fueled vehicles, starting in 1998.

The Antelope Valley School District in southern California tested an electric bus that had been built by Blue Bird and Westinghouse. The tests were sponsored by the air pollution control district. The electric bus scored well in all categories except range, limited by battery capacity to 75 to 80 miles. Blue Bird literature, describing the bus, noted that nearly half the school bus routes in the United States were less than its 80-mile range. Preliminary studies showed that diesel fuel was cheaper and easier to obtain, although it was less desirable from an environmental perspective. Blue Bird also issued literature featuring its natural gas-powered school buses, which could be powered by John Deere, Cummins, Hercules, or General Motors power plants.

The tour bus industry is thriving, with over 600 members in the National Tour Association, the trade group. Some tour companies own buses, others charter them, serving a market that consists mainly of senior citizens. Promotional materials note: "The typical tour traveler is 65 years or older." Nearly all the tour buses are luxurious, foreign-built makes, but there are also a few older buses, such as the bright red double-decked Leylands, imported from England.

A European merger that would eventually impact U.S. markets occurred in 1995, when Mercedes-Benz and Kässbohrer joined. One of their products is the Setra bus, used in the United States for tours.

An articulated Nova bus, used in the Toronto area. The Nova firm is located in St-Eustache, Quebec, and Roswell, New Mexico. *Nova Bus Corporation*

Much of the history of the bus industry has dealt with mergers and consolidations, a trend that continued into the 1990s, as a firm called Coach USA began acquiring major tour and charter bus operations throughout the nation. According to the April 1997 issue of *National Bus Trader* magazine, the acquiring company had "identified the motorcoach industry as ripe for consolidation, and began to screen a large number of bus operations. Requirements included sizable operations, profitability, a long track record, clean ownership structure, demonstrated industry leadership and entrepreneurial management." As many as 225 motorcoach companies were initially screened, and by 1995 Coach USA had acquired six firms, operating a total of 760 coaches. Since then, Coach USA has taken over 10 more companies and, by early 1997, controlled 1,700 coaches. Larry Plachno, who wrote the *National Bus Trader* article, said:

> There is an interesting correlation here, because Greyhound in the 1930s and Coach USA today both represent the major effort at consolidation, and hence effectively could pick and choose their merger partners. In other areas, the consolidations are substantially different. Greyhound concentrated on scheduled intercity bus service and on obtaining missing but needed routes. Coach USA has so far avoided getting involved with long-distance scheduled intercity bus service, and instead has concentrated on the charter and tour market, as well as contract and privatized commuter and transit service.

Buses, like many other vehicles, have been featured on the "big screen." In 1994, a dowdy 1967 General Motors transit bus was featured in the movie *Speed*, starring Keanu Reeves and Sandra Bullock. In the movie, a bomb in the bus was set to explode if the vehicle's speed dropped below 50 miles per hour. As a result, moviegoers got to see the old bus move with an unaccustomed hustle. (When the movie was first shown on TV in 1996, a woman won the bus in a phone-in contest. In 1997 she reportedly sold it to a southern California restaurant, Planet Hollywood.)

In a 1997 movie, *The Apostle*, for which actor Robert Duvall received an Oscar nomination for his portrayal of a dynamic, Bible-thumping Southern pastor, a circa-1950 Chevrolet ex-school bus played a prominent role. As the pastor was trying to organize a new congregation in a small Louisiana town, he used the brightly painted bus to pick up parishioners and deliver them to church.

An article in the November/December issue of *School Bus Fleet* told about southern California firms that supply buses for use in the movies. The old buses are bought at auctions and repainted. Filmmakers try to keep them authentic, although the comment was made that all the safety mirrors on school buses make them difficult to use in filming because if a light hits a mirror, the camera is blinded.

During this decade, John Madden, the former Oakland Raiders coach and probably the nation's foremost pro football commentator, used a bus to travel from game site to game site. This was because of his intense dislike of flying. In some radio markets, he would also have a daily sports

A 1992 TMC, which was one of 14 ethanol-powered buses used in Peoria. TMC stands for Transportation Manufacturing Corporation. Greater Peoria Mass Transit District

commentary, which sometimes would originate from the traveling bus.

Here's some fairly current statistics regarding school buses and their use. *School Bus Fleet* magazine's December 1997 issue gave a listing of the nation's 100 largest school bus fleets for 1997. The 10 largest (with number of buses in parentheses) are New York Public Schools (4,345); Los Angeles County Unified School District (2,740); Chicago Public Schools (2,231); Dade County (Florida) Public Schools (1,951); Broward County (Florida) School Board (1,409); Milwaukee Public Schools (1,400); Houston Independent School District (1,350); Dallas County Schools (1,270); Hillsborough County (Florida) District (1,260); and Fairfax County (Virginia) Public Schools (1,245). Of the 10 just listed, 5 ran all their own buses; 3 relied completely on buses supplied and run by outside contractors; and 2 relied partially on outside contractors. The magazine estimated that the nation's entire 1996 school bus fleet totaled about 413,000 buses, and carried over 20 million pupils per day. Laidlaw Transit was the largest private contractor, operating over 38,000 buses.

Today's buses are reaping the benefits of modern technology. Global positioning systems (GPS) which rely on earth satellites to calculate one's exact loca-

tion, are being introduced into bus operations. One public transit operator uses the device to trigger "next stop" announcements on a bus. An article in the March 1998 issue of *School Bus Fleet* said that in the fall of 1998, a school bus operator in Bemidji, Minnesota, working in conjunction with the local telephone company, will have a GPS-based system that will telephone the parents' home five minutes before the school bus will arrive.

The number of bus manufacturers is quite large, with a mix of those that are nationally known, to those less known serving regional markets. *Metro Magazine*, in its July/August 1998 issue, contained a list of shuttle bus builders. Firms listed included Advanced Vehicle Systems, Arcola Special Vehicles, Blue Bird, Champion Motor Coach, Chance Coach, Inc., Craftsmen Limousine Inc., Curtis Coach & Equipment; Diamond Coach Corp., Dina/MCI, ElDorado National, ElDorado National-Michigan, Electric Vehicles International, Federal Coach, Gillig Corp., Goshen Coach, Krystal Koach, Mathews Specialty Vehicles, Mauck Special Vehicles, Metrotrans, Mid Bus Inc., New Flyer of America, Neoplan, Nova BUS, Orion Bus Industries, Seven O Seven Industries, Inc., Shepard Bros., Stratus Specialty Vehicles, Supreme Corp., Thomas Built Buses,

A 1993 Flxible with vinyl wrap used for advertising a local newspaper. *Broward County Mass Transit Division*

Trolley Enterprises Inc., Turtle Top, Van Hool, and Word Trans. Interestingly, only a few of these have been mentioned elsewhere in this text, which may be indicative of the fast turnover in new builders. In the medium-size bus industry, many of the firms also build motor homes, utilizing the same shell.

As for larger buses, Larry Plachno, in the *National Bus Trader* March 1998 issue, wrote:

> The increasing importance of tour operations and decreasing importance of scheduled service will be reflected in the type of vehicles we will operate in the future. At one point, the needs of Greyhound and Trailways dominated bus design and we built a "Sherman tank" type of vehicle that could operate profitably in scheduled service from New York to San Francisco in the snow, rain, sleet and whatever else Mother Nature could come up with. In more recent years, a portion of the industry has been moving more toward European type buses, which tend to have more styling appeal and passenger amenities, but less overall longevity.

U.S.-built school buses are sometimes exported. An article in the March 11, 1998, issue of *The Journal of Commerce* said, in part:

> U.S.-made school buses are turning up in some pretty unlikely places around the world. But few of these buses will ever be used to carry students to school. Rather, most are being sold to companies that use them to transport workers to and from the job site, whether that's a factory or a field where crops are being tended and harvested.

Most of the exported buses are sent in a disassembled state, and assembled in the importing nation, thereby benefiting from lower duties. One vessel operator noted that bus exports from the United States were dropping because of increased competition from buses built in Eastern Europe and China.

APTA estimates that in 1995, local transit buses boarded about 4.9 billion passengers annually, down from the figure for 1990. *Metro Magazine*, in its September/October 1997 issue, listed the largest transit bus fleets in the United States. The largest was MTA New York City Transit, with 3,745 buses. In descending order were New Jersey Transit Corp. (2,970 buses); Los Angeles County MTA (2,020); Chicago Transit Authority (1,930); Southeastern Pennsylvania Transportation Authority (1,336); Washington Metropolitan Area Transit Authority (1,285); King County Metro (Seattle, 1,234 buses); Metropolitan Transit Authority of Harris County (Houston, 1,179 buses); New York City Department of Transportation (1,094); and Massachusetts Bay Transportation Authority (1,029).

A 1994 Ford used as a shuttle bus at the Kansas City, Missouri, airport. Many buses used at airports had U-shaped seating. *Kansas City Aviation Department*

As the century ends, no common bus has emerged, but highly specialized buses have developed for markets of different sizes and situations. Twenty-five years ago, it was predicted that mass transit would increase astronomically, leaving the automobile trailing in the dust. That has yet to happen. The role of the bus continues to be that of secondary transportation, providing a service when we can't use our automobiles.

A 30-foot Gillig used in Peoria. *Greater Peoria Mass Transit District*

Next Page
The transportation office at Kent State University made this bus look like a rocket. Toward the rear, note a folded wing. Just how high the rig could fly was not specified. *Kent State University*

Baltimore/Washington International Airport uses 20 of these National shuttle buses, powered by compressed natural gas. The 23-passenger buses are equipped with Hercules six-cylinder turbo-powered natural gas vehicle engines. *Baltimore/Washington International Airport*

A small Collins school bus body on a mid-1990s Chevrolet chassis. Buses of this size are used for light runs or for carrying disabled students. In 1995, sales of school buses on van chassis totaled 5,854 units, out of a total of 36,386 school bus sales. School buses on conventional truck chassis, with the engine ahead of the cab, totaled 20,861 units, and buses with the driver at the front totaled 9,671 units. The Collins firm is located in South Hutchinson, Kansas. *Collins Bus Corp.*

An electric bus being tested at Los Angeles International Airport. It was manufactured by the Specialty Vehicle Manufacturing Corporation of Downey, California. *Los Angeles Department of Airports*

A 1996 Nova with vinyl wrap advertising a showing at the Knoxville Museum of Art. *Knoxville Area Transit*

This is one of an order of 400 transit buses that North American Bus Industries delivered to the Southeastern Pennsylvania Transportation Authority between 1995 and 1997. The buses are equipped with a prerecorded, next-stop announcement system, which is triggered by global-positioning satellites. North American Bus Industries has its U.S. headquarters and assembly operation in Anniston, Alabama. The firm is controlled by Hungarian interests and builds many components in Budapest. North American Bus Industries

A Cobus, built in Germany by Contrac GmbH, used to shuttle passengers at Los Angeles International Airport. It rides close to the ground and several large doors allow passengers to exit quickly. Capacity is 140 passengers—both seated and standing. Los Angeles Department of Airports

A 1997 Gillig bus, powered by natural gas, is being tested in parking lot shuttle service at the Los Angeles International Airport. Currently, Gillig is not building school buses. Los Angeles Department of Airports

A 1997 low-floor Gillig, operated by Broward County Transit in Florida. Note the ramp. *Broward County Mass Transit Division*

This 1997 Nova RTS is used in Detroit. *Nova Bus Corp.*

This Orion is used in New York City. The Orion firm is headquartered in Mississauga, Ontario, but assembles buses destined to its U.S. customers in Oriskany, New York. *Orion Bus Industries*

Setra buses are a well-known European make, which began selling in the United States in the mid-1980s. The firm recently became associated with Mercedes-Benz. Current ads stress German engineering, European styling, and an American power-train. Setra

Prevost buses were first built in 1924. The firm is located in Sainte Claire, Quebec, and is affiliated with Volvo and with Henlys Group (in the UK). This is one of its current buses, the 45-foot LeMirage XL45 "Entertainer," engineered for "professional entertainers seeking the ultimate in travel quarters with the best in sleeping comfort, balanced weight distribution, and ample underfloor storage . . ." Prevost

This is one of three passenger transfer vehicles placed into use at the Philadelphia International Airport in 1998. Each can accommodate 125 passengers. The body can be elevated to match the aircraft's height. The vehicles are 60 feet long and can travel at 30 miles per hour. The manufacturer is Tecksol, a firm with operations in both Sainte-Foy, Quebec, and Hagerstown, Maryland. Philadelphia International Airport

BIBLIOGRAPHY

Bibliography

A Nation in Motion (Washington, DC: U.S. D.O.T., 1976).

Abbit, Jerry W., *History of Transit in the Valley of the Sun, 1887–1989* (Phoenix: The City of Phoenix Transit System, 1990).

APTA 1997 Transit Fact Book (Washington, DC: American Public Transit Association, 1997).

A. J. Brosseau, *The Field of the Motor Bus* (New York: National Automobile Chamber of Commerce, 1927).

Brown, Lester R., Christopher Flavin, and Colin Norman, *The Future of the Automobile in an Oil-Short World* (Washington, DC: Worldwatch Institute, 1979).

Burby, John, *The Great American Motion Sickness, or Why You Can't Get There From Here* (Boston: Little, Brown, 1971).

Burness, Tad, *American Truck & Bus Spotter's Guide 1920–1985* (Osceola: Motorbooks International, 1985).

Bus Operating Practice (New York: Mack Trucks, Inc., 1925).

The Bus Pages, recent editions (McMinnville, OR: Bus Book Publishing, Inc.).

Carson, Clayborne, "The Montgomery Story: How a Southern Bus Boycott Changed America Forever," *San Francisco Examiner Magazine* (February 2, 1997), pp. 8–17.

Cost of Service of the Jitney Bus (New York: American Electric Railroad Association, 1915).

Covert, Timon, "Rural Education and the School Bus," *Graham Bros. [truck and bus] Vocational Folders* (Detroit), 1926, pp. 4–7.

Crismon, Frederick W., *International Trucks* (Osceola: MBI Publishing Company, 1995).

Daniel, J. M., *Hackney: The History of a Company* (Wilson, N.C.: the company, 1979).

Denison, Merrill, *The Power to Go* (New York: Doubleday, 1956).

The Dependable Diesel (a magazine published by Cummins Engine Company), 1950s issues.

Farris, Martin T., and Forrest E. Harding, *Passenger Transportation* (Englewood Cliffs, NJ: Prentice Hall, 1976).

Fellmeth, Robert, *The Interstate Commerce Omission* [sic] (New York: Grossman, 1970).

Firestone, Harvey S., Jr. *Man on the Move* (New York: Putnam's, 1967).

Gannon, James P., "The Bus Set," in *Passenger Transportation*, Stanley C. Hollander, editor (East Lansing, MI: Michigan State University, 1968), pp. 271–276.

Georgano, G. N., *The Complete Encyclopedia of Commercial Vehicles* (Iola, WI: Krause, 1979).

Get on to Something Great (Washington, D.C.: National Association of Motor Bus Owners, 1974).

Golden Years of Highway Transportation, (50th Anniversary Issue of *Commercial Car Journal*, Philadelphia: September 1961).

Grover, Cornell A., and Carolyn S. Grover, "The Teton Stage Lines," *Snake River Echoes* (Rexburg, Idaho: Upper Snake River Valley Historical Society, 1984), pp. 19–21.

Horine, Merrill C., "The Bus Body and the Laws of Forty-Eight States Affecting It," *The Automobile Trimmer and Painter* (July 1926), pp. 36–38.

Horner, Frederick C., *The Application of Motor Trans-*

port to the Movement of Freight and Passengers (New York: National Automobile Chamber of Commerce, 1929).

Howley, Tim, "1948 Greyhound Silversides Bus," *Special-Interest Autos* (March/April 1997), pp. 36–43, 69.

Intercity Buses at War (Washington, D.C.: National Association of Motor Bus Operators, ca. 1943).

Jacobs, David, *American Buses —Greyhound, Trailways and Urban Transportation* (London: Osprey, 1985).

Keilty, Edmund, *The Short Line Doodlebug* (Glendale, CA: Interurban Press, 1988).

Kelly, Richard, "Custom Bus Bodies, how they got to school back then," *Special-Interest Autos* (July/August 1995), pp. 42–45.

Kulp, Randolph L., editor, *History of Mack Rail Motor Cars and Locomotives* (Allentown, PA: Lehigh Valley Chapter, National Railway Historical Society, Inc., 1971).

Lichtanski, Frank J., "Monterey Peninsula Transit," *Motor Coach Age* (January 1980), pp. 4–24.

Lidz, Jane, *Rolling Homes, Handmade Houses on Wheels* (New York: A & W Visual Library, 1979).

Lifelines: How Trucks and Buses Serve America (Detroit: Motor Vehicle Manufacturers Association, 1980).

Luna, Charles, *The UTU Handbook of Transportation in America* (New York: Popular Library, 1971).

"Mack Bus," *Motor Coach Age* (March/April, 1974) based on materials abstracted from John B. Montville's book *Mack* (Newfoundland, NJ: Haessner Publishing Co., 1973).

Making Bus Operations Pay (New York: McGraw-Hill, 1932).

McMillan, A. G., *Model A/AA Ford Truck Owner* reprints of sales materials distributed to Ford dealers circa 1930 (Arcadia, CA: Post-Era Books, 1975).

Meier, Albert E., and John P. Hoschek, *Over the Road: A History of Intercity Bus Transportation in the United States* (Upper Montclair, NJ: Motor Bus Society: 1975).

The Motor Bus as a Medium of Passenger Transportation (Detroit: Packard Motor Car Company, 1921).

Motor Coach Age, various issues.

Motor Trucks in the Metropolis (New Haven: Wilbur Smith and Associates, 1969).

Mroz, Albert, *The Illustrated Encyclopedia of American Trucks and Commercial Vehicles* (Iola, WI: Krause, 1996).

National Bus Trader, current issues.

NTA Today (Lexington, KY: National Tour Association, Inc., 1986).

Paddle, The (newsletter published by the Pacific Bus Museum), current issues.

"Pickwick Develops Duplex Bus," *Automotive Industries* (May 17, 1930), pp. 772–773.

Plachno, Larry, *Modern Intercity Coaches* (Polo, IL: Transportation Trails, 1997).

Redden, Robert, *Buses: Their History*, a videotape, circa-1987.

Rose, Albert C., *Historic American Roads* (New York: Crown, 1976).

Schindler, Manfred, *Otto Kässbohrer—His Views and Achievements in an Era of Change* (Ulm, Germany: Karl Kässbohrer Fahrzeugwerke GmbH, 1979).

School Bus Fleet, current issues.

Silver Book, various years.

Standard Military Motor Vehicles, TM 9-2800 (Washington, DC: War Department, 1943)—reprinted by Portrayal Press, Bloomfield, NJ.

Stauss, Ed, *The Bus World Encyclopedia of Buses* (Woodland Hills, CA: Stauss Publications, 1988).

Taxation of Motor Vehicle Transportation (New York: National Industrial Conference Board, 1932).

The Taxi Project: Realistic Solutions for Today (New York: The Museum of Modern Art, 1976).

Thomas, D. H., *The Southwestern Indian Detours* (Phoenix: Hunter, 1978).

Vehicle Catalog, Volumes 1 and 2 (Washington, DC: U.S. D.O.T., 1990).

Whalen, Grover, *Replacing Street Cars With Motor Buses* (New York: National Automobile Chamber of Commerce, 1920).

Wood, Donald F., "Bringing 'Em Back to School," *Old Car News & Marketplace* (August 30, 1990), p. 70. *Commercial Trucks* (Osceola, WI : MBI Publishing Company, 1993). "Open for Business," *Special-interest Autos*, No. 53 (1979), pp. 32–37.

Wren, James A., and Genevieve J. Wren, *Motor Trucks of America* (Ann Arbor: University of Michigan Press, 1979).

INDEX